"Every man should be skilled in the art of drinking tea, drinking liquor, eating and making love".....

- Lisu motto

II

PEOPLE OF THE HILLS

by

PREECHA CHATURABHAWD

LAYOUT AND EDITING:
ALAN R. RANDALL

IV

Siam Square, G.P.O. Box 427, Bangkok, Thailand.

ISBN 974-210-313-5

VI

CONTENTS

INTRODUCTION

The peoples who form the varied hill tribes of northern Thailand are attracting more and more attention from visitors from overseas. It is not because the area is well-known as a source of the opium poppy, but rather because the diverse lives that these people live-- out show an increasingly materialistic world that riches and the possessions that money buys are not the source of happiness.

Happiness is a state of mind, something that is beyond price - and these hill people, poor though they may be in material things, live a life that can honestly be called "happy". The artifacts they produce are being made known to an increasing number of people through the Tribal Research Centre in Chiang Mai, and through the growing number of outlets where a visitor may purchase some of the intricate things produced, be they of cloth, wood or metal.

Most studies of the peoples who live in the rather cool hills of northern Thailand have either tended to concentrate on the products made by the hill folk or else they have been rather studious anthropological or sociological tomes which, however well-intentioned, do somehow try and dissect the people as would a doctor at a postmortem!

The present book uses neither of these approaches, but rather the author has tried, both in words and through photographs, to give an objective view of the daily lives of these fascinating people. Their customs, to be sure, are rather different from those of the Westerner - especially when it comes to sexual matters. But you will find a great honesty in their way of living. They are not prigs or prudes, but happy with their simple way of living, based as it so often is on centuries of tradition.

They have, as you will see, no desires for the dubious "delights" of the West. The government is trying to help them to change their farming crops - and the leader in this gigantic task is H.M. the King of Thailand who spares no efforts to assist these members of the nation he reigns so benignly over.

It is felt that you will be delighted and fascinated by reading of ways of living so different from the norm. The book demands of the reader but one thing - an open mind. Then perhaps you will get a glimpse of that most elusive of states - the state we call in English "Happiness".

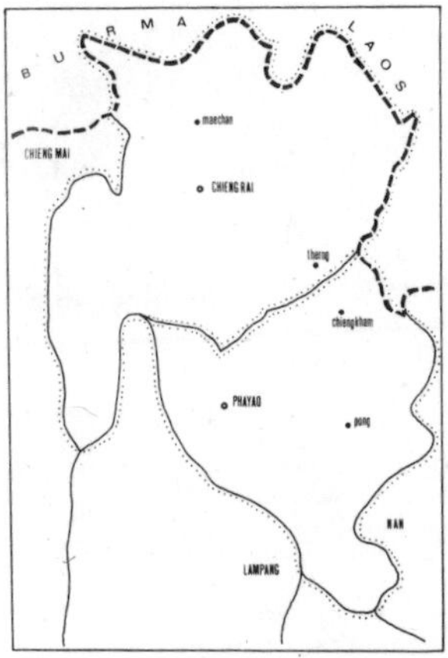

Total of villages :	*105*
Total of households :	*3,056*
Total population :	*22,652*

YAO

The hilltribe people of Thailand are primitive in nature. To many sociologists, anthropologists and even casual visitors, their simplicity is a relief from the social tensions and complexities of urban living.

Their cultures and mode of living run parallel with deep-rooted beliefs in ancestor worship, animism and spirit worship - sometimes interlaced as a result of missionary work with a little Buddhism or Christianity. These practices govern every aspect of their sexual, marital, family and economic life.

This first section will deal with the Yao, whose life is intrinsically linked with the worship of spirits, so much so that a simple problem becomes unman-

A Yao bride in traditional dress before leaving for the groom's village.

A painting on the cover of a Yao passport

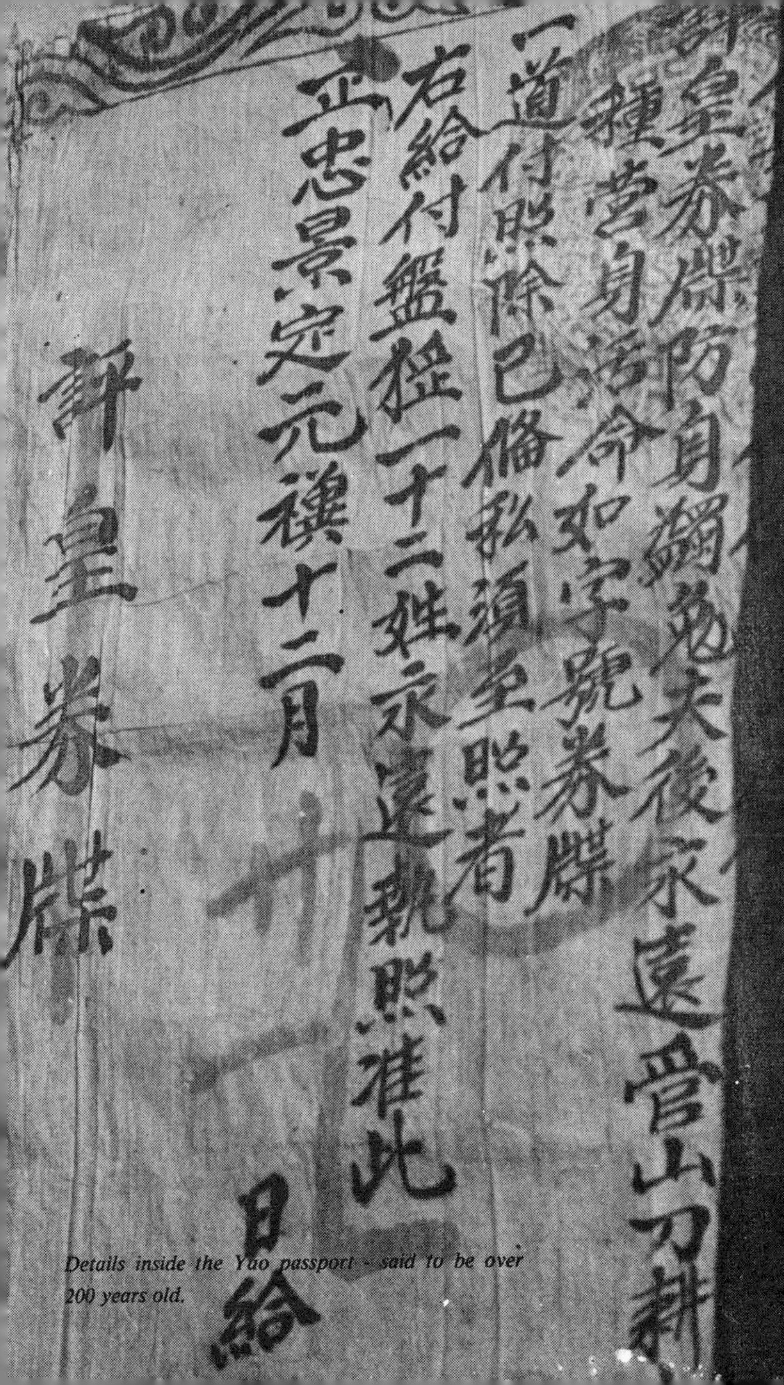

皇券牒防身蹈免夫役永遠營山刀耕
種營身活命如字號券牒
一道付照除已備私須至照者
右給付盤徭一十二姓永遠執照准此
正忠景定元禩十二月
日給
評皇券牒

Details inside the Yao passport - said to be over 200 years old.

A view of a Yao village. This one can be reached by car, but most are only accessible on foot.

nageable without an oracle's divination. Spirits dominate a person's life even before they are born.

The Yao once inhabited parts of central China in the provinces of Tzechuan, Kieng-tsi and adjoining areas. They were disturbed by hostile neighbours and migrated south, settling in areas now forming parts of Burma, Laos, Vietnam and Thailand. In Thailand they are found in some Northern provinces, expecially in mountainous areas of Chiang Rai, Chiang Mai, Lampang and Mae Hong Son. Some occasionally venture to the markets in the towns and villages of these provinces.

Because of the past close relationship with the Chinese, they have adopted Chinese customs and traditions to suit their way of life. The two races have similar facial features, only language and dress differ.

The Yao migrated into Thailand through Burma and Laos between 1910 and 1950. They

A typical Yao house with tiled roof. The bamboo water conduit can be seen passing the house.

These conduits clearly seen right, carry water to every house in as village.

have made their homes in mountain ranges about 3,000 to 4,000 feet above sea level in areas where there is a natural water supply suitable for cultivation

'Biew-Lahm' or barn-like building seen in every Yao village. It's clumsy shape and small size makes it seem like a doll's house.

and livestock raising and near a forest with considerable bamboo clumps.

Housing

The Yaos usually build their simple huts mainly from bamboo. Timber is used for support poles only. Roofing is of the most suitable material to hand. It may be ya-kha (thatch), split bamboo, palm leaves, or thin sheets of light-weight wood, about 8 inches by four to six inches. The poles are either partly sunk into the ground or simply erected on it. The roof edges are kept low so that they almost reach the ground. This protects the inside of the houses from wind and rain. The floors are left uncovered, except for the sleeping areas which are both walled and floored. These are so small that they are just big enough to sleep in. These "rooms" are actually platforms partitioned with bamboo sheets to form a row of small, doorless closets.

A Yao girl in full dress

Turban styles vary. This one popular in Laos and in areas near the border has 'rabbit's ears'.

(Left) An unusual sight - a Yao girl without her head dress. Usually a girl will only take off her turban in her bedroom at night.

The unfloored part of the house is used for all other purposes, such as receiving visitors and as a common room. A fire burns in this section throughout the year. This is used for boiling water to make tea and for lighting water–pipes for smok–

Above: A mother acts as her daughter's beautician by plucking the downy-like hairs from the forehead. Many Chinese follow this practice.

ing. Short-legged stools or logs are provided for people to sit on. Hung from the ceiling above the fire is a bamboo tray, said to symbolize the Yao's home. This tray is used for storing fern seeds, tobacco leaves, dried bamboo sprouts, dried vegetables, hides, salt etc.

Traditionally, there are three fireplaces in each house. The second being used for cooking food and the third for preparing animal feedstuffs.

Yao girls feeding their swine

Food

The Yaos' staple food is rice. It is a special variety which is grown on the mountain slopes. When properly cooked this type of rice is thought tastier than rice grown on the plains and is both more tender and "sappier". It is sometimes mistaken for glutinous rice (kow nee-oh). The rice is eaten from a small, glazed earthenware bowl with bamboo chopsticks, sometimes coloured.

The eating table is of woven bamboo, circular shaped. This table is placed on the floor and people sit around it on their stools or logs to eat. Dogs, pigs and chickens have the full run of this part of the house and are usually on hand at meal times to get tit-bits.

The Yao prepare an alcoholic drink from maize, paddy, millet or wheat, home grown. The brew is very potent and its taste is characterized by the ingredients used. It is sometimes drunk before meals.

Besides rice, Yao diet includes pork, pumpkin, potatoes and other root vegetables and well as chilli and salt. When it is an occasion of paying

The Yao brew a very potent liquor. Maize, rice, sticky or ordinary, or wheat are used as the base. Illustrated is the still.

respect to the spirits, chicken is also served - a practice similar to the Chinese.

Dress

Yao women dress well. They wear black slacks and blouses embroidered with beautiful designs.

A Yao man seen writing greetings. The Yao are the only hill tribe to read and write Chinese.

Above : One offering tray has gold and silver paper, the other holds a cooked chicken.

Yao are skilled in working both gold and silver. This old man is seen making ornaments to adorn the women.

Two Yao men making 'money' with a tool shown above. The ink is made from burnt straw ash.

A wooden block carved with figures of horses used in printing gold and silver 'money' for offering to the spirits. The horses signify the mode of transporting the money to the heavens.

The neck of the blouse is edged with a long pink "puff". They also wear turbans and lengths of coloured cloth around the waist. During festivals, they add ornaments that make them appear almost over-adorned, including suspending long puffs, strips of silver and coins of many denominations. At the edge of the blouse are hung small tinkling bells. The blouses are easily made and look like calf length gowns. Yao women wear no underwear, and the mode of dressing is the same for young and old alike. The material used is heavyweight and does not change with the seasonal temperature.

A Yao man will wear black trousers and a black coat. The trousers are similar to those worn by the Shan, and the coat like that of the Chinese. The edge of the coat is often embroidered and the shoulders have silver buttons. Formerly Yao men wore peakless caps and their hair in pig-tail style, but the younger generation do not favour these.

Followers of the senior witch-doctor dancing at the ceremony honouring 'Farm-ching', which Yao believe, can protect them from harm.

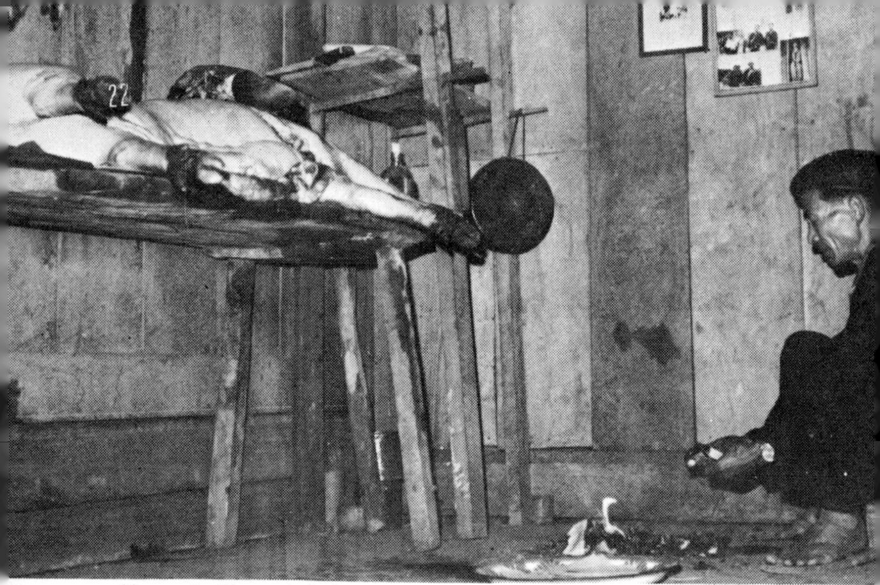

Above: A village witch-doctor prays to the ancestors' spirits before the sacrificial offering of a whole pig. Gold and silver paper is being burned in traditional Chinese style.

Below: A slaughtered pig is the offering here.

This Yao man is chanting from a Chinese script manuscript. In front of him is a pig's head - his offering to the spirits of his ancestors.

Spirit worship

Like most hill tribes, Yao respect all spirits – including those of their ancestors, the sky, the wind and the forest. They believe that these spirits can protect them and bring prosperity. Homage is paid to the spirits on many occasions, for example when crops are abundant or when there is sickness. Spirits are also invoked before making a journey. All these ceremonies involve the killing of pigs and poultry as offerings to the spirits.

The most influential people in any group of the tribe are the practitioners of witchcraft, since the spirits play such an important part in daily

Above: A senior Yao witch-doctor performing a rite.

Below: The assistant witch-doctor at a rite near a spirit house.

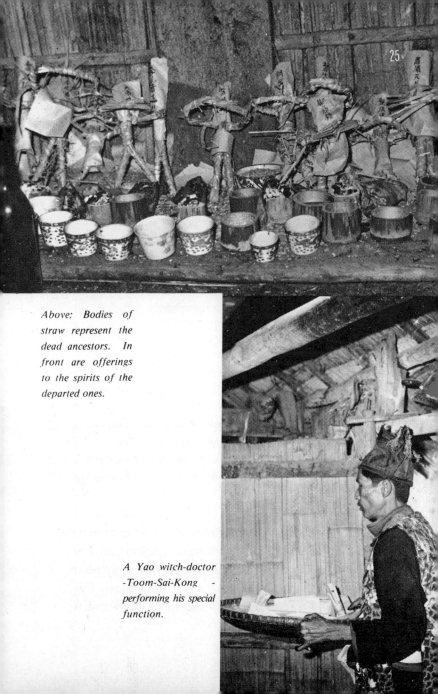

Above: Bodies of straw represent the dead ancestors. In front are offerings to the spirits of the departed ones.

A Yao witch-doctor -Toom-Sai-Kong - performing his special function.

The entrance to a Yao house with woven bamboo hung at the entrance. This signifies that there is a sick person in the house and no one is permitted to enter. The woven bamboo 'protects the sick from bad spirits' and is left in place for at least seven days.

living from birth to death. When sick, Yao prefer the witch-doctor to modern medicines. Only if this form of treatment fails are modern drugs tried. There are two types of witch-doctor-the *toom sai kong* who takes care of the great spirit and the *sai ton,* who looks after smaller rituals. The former group require a thorough knowledge of their craft.

A group of Yao will make many offerings to the spirits during the course of a year. For these, each family must hold a stock of straw paper. This is used to represent gold and silver leaves and is burnt at the offering. They make this special type of paper themselves from the pulp of some varieties of soft-wood trees found in nearby forests.

Sexual mores

Yao people are very free and open in sexual matters and such a word as "rape" has no place in their language. As early as the age of 14 or 15 Yao young boys and girls will court instinctively and openly. A marriage is not a necessity for lovers

A decorated imitation bridge. When a person in a Yao village falls ill, such a construction is built as it is believed that the bridge will be used as a symbol of happiness and that the sick person's life will be extended by his recovery.

to live together as man and wife. Traditionally it is not even improper behaviour for a woman to go from one lover to another. This type of woman is always welcomed by the man's parents and vice versa. It is by no means uncommon for a woman

The spirit shrine to be seen in every Yao house. Joss paper and other items are kept on the lower shelf.

Above: A Yao woman returns from the fields. Both her own and the horse's back are laden with produce.

Below: It is Yao custom to keep rice on the stalk, bringing it out as they require to use it. A youngster is seen drying rice on a high platform.

to have a number of illegitimate children when she goes to live with her new lover. It is traditional that if a girl becomes pregnant while living with a particular man he has to pay a fine of 40 baht (US$2) plus a chicken, to the headman of the village.

While free love is not, as was seen, uncommon, there are also ceremonial weddings full of rites and rituals.

A side view of the bridal head-dress.

Guests at a Yao wedding feast. The bride, in a different head-dress serves the guests.

Marriage

The preliminaries for a wedding begin with the groom and a group of kinsmen contacting the girl's parents to ask their permission. This group has to agree *sinsord* (money to be paid to the bride's parents at the time of the wedding). This amounts to a sum of between 2,000 baht and 3,200 baht (US$100 to US$160), and is often paid in silver ingots. Besides *sinsord,* the groom's party will have to provide up to four pigs and an adequate supply of alcoholic drink for the reception.

According to custom, *sinsord* is either paid at the time of the contract or by instalment over a three or four year period depending upon the demands of the prospective bride's parents. If a child is born to the parents before *sinsord* is cleared, the child can be given to the wife's parents to clear the debt. Sometimes the child is even sold in order that the husband can pay the outstanding amount.

Far left: Yao musical instruments. Left to right : cymbals 'Jao'; a gong 'Mung' and a drum 'Hoey'

Left: A flute-type musical instrument - 'Hyatt' in Yao.

There are cases where the wife's parents will waive any payment.

The wedding agreement is usually written. It will stipulate the amount of *sinsord,* the number of animals to be slaughtered for the feast, the number of guests to be invited by each side and, if necessary, a special sum of money for the girl's parents to return to their home after the ceremony.

The actual ceremony begins at a time chosen as auspicious for the event. The bride's parents take the girl in procession to the groom's village – if she lives in another village. She does not go to her future husband's house but rests overnight at a relative's or friend's house. The groom's group send musicians to welcome the bridal procession at the outskirts of his village. Drinks are served to the bridal party and a reception honouring the parents is arranged for that evening at the groom's house. Musicians are again sent to invite the parents to the party. At the reception the bride's parents are seated separately from other guests and all are entertained with traditional music.

During the initial ceremony, the future bride has to be veiled and is not permitted to enter the man's house through the front way. The tribe maintains that such action would be a bad omen as the girl still respects her own spirits.

On the second day of the celebrations, two special guests are invited to be seated with the girl's parents. These are the match-makers - one male and one female. Usually more guests are invited for

The design on one side of the cloth embroidered by a Yao bride for her prospective husband.

Above: The New Year is the time for bangs. Here a Yao man is loading his home-made rifle with gunpowder.

Left: A sow seems unperturbed by exploding fire crackers. These are made by packing gunpowder tightly into a bamboo joint and sinking one part into the ground. The bursting sound may be likened to that of a rocket firing.

this second day of festivities. These may include people from other villages as well as government officials. At the auspicious time for the wedding, usually at nightfall on this second day, the bride is brought to stand by the groom at the groom's house, with all the relatives and friends in attendance. Sometimes the bridal couple have to stand for hours bowing each time the witch-doctor ends a passage of incantations. The guests, meanwhile, have placed their presents on a table and have been served food and drink. Each guest in turn pours a drop of liquor into a special cup as their offering to their special spirits.

The invitation to attend such a wedding reception is made by sending a small package of salt

It looks like an apron, but is part of a Yao girl's special attire for the New Year. It can adorn the shoulders or be worn around the waist.

to each person to be invited. Messengers attach the package of salt to the wall of the house when no one is at home. Those attending the reception have to show their "invitation card" - the package of salt! A person unable to attend returns his package immediately. Late at night, at the end of the reception, the bride and groom are accompanied to their room where they receive their presents and other offerings.

Pregnancy and child birth

Medical care, even in the primative tribal form, is completely ignored in prenatal cases. Instead, the husband, knowing of the imminence of

Offerings to the spirits of the ancestors - liquor, food and uncooked rice.

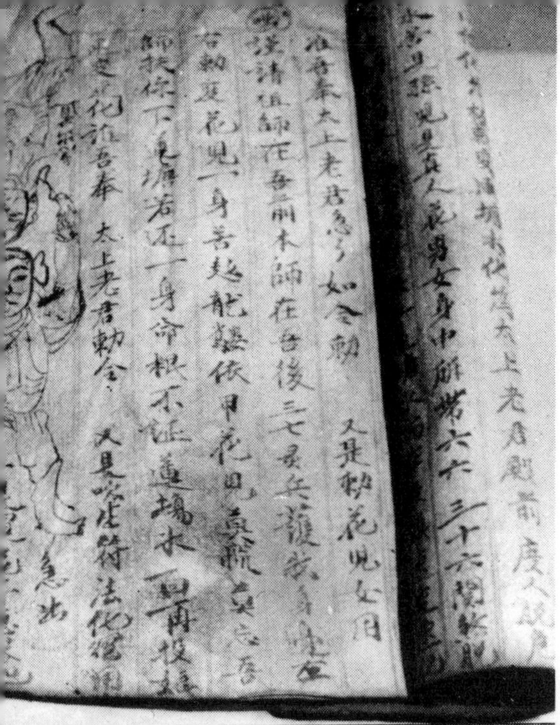

Two photos of the sacred book of the Yao which, is is claimed, help a pregnant woman through the difficult stages of child birth. The witch-doctor chants the Chinese text and burns copies of the drawings he has made on paper.

Bamboo 'trees' with steamed sticky rice in banana leaves, all joined with 'holy' thread - another type of offering.

the birth, quickly makes offerings to the spirit of the house – known as *Sam Dao* – and implores for help. He asks that his wife be strong for the coming ordeal, that the child be healthy and free from any deformity and that both mother and child will enjoy general well–being. Then he virtually turns the house into a hospital for the delivery.

Firstly, the floor of the house, usually at a corner, is raised to make a platform. At the side of the platform large amounts of straw are scattered and clean cloths are placed. Above the platform a rope is securely tied to the ceiling. According to tribal beliefs this is for the woman in labour to pull to summon sufficient delivery wind at the critical time seconds before the birth. This practice was also common among Thais in olden times. Then the husband asks the village midwife, usually an aunt, or anyone who has helped deliver a child previously, to be on hand.

When the baby is safely delivered, the midwife lays it on the straw and, using a knife made of bamboo, cuts off the umbilical cord. This is later put into a basket and tied on a tree to dry out naturally.

Blessing rites for the new-born child are usually held three days after its birth and the father will invite the witch-doctor to conduct them. Offerings at such a ceremony include five cups of liquor, a cup of drinking water, a silver rupee, a piece of white cloth, a half kilogram of rice wrapped in white cloth and a large fowl of any colour except white. During this ceremony the child receives his (or her) first bath and hears his (or her) first lullaby. Uttered by the witch-doctor holding the baby in his arms the lullaby is the chanting of sacred scriptures and usually lasts for more than an hour.

Encroachment into the ritual perimeter while this ceremony is in progress is strictly prohibited. Should any person - male or female - cross the area, they are considered a "wandering parent" of the baby and will be held responsible for the child's future well-being. For example, when the child becomes sick, the person would be brought to pray for the child's recovery!

At the ending of the blessing rites, the father and the witch–doctor celebrate by eating dinner together and consuming - usually - large amounts of liquor. Among the dishes served at the dinner is fowl. This is considered most important in that, while eating it, the witch–doctor reads the tongue and leg bones of the bird to predict the luck of the child. If the tongue curves inwards, the omens are good - the child will gain ascendancy and be the comfort of his parents. A row of zigzag holes

The witch-doctor's instruments are always at the ready. Seen here are a crowned dagger, flags and a water buffalo horn.

in the leg bone forbodes that the child will live a destitute life and be a burden to his parents.

During the first four to seven days after delivery of the child, the mother is confined to the house and bathes only in medicinal herbal water. She is forbidden to drink cold water, eat cold food or pickles, the meat of barking deer, ox, water buffalo or scale-less fish as such food could cause her womb to contract leaving her unable to bear any more children. Finally, she must desist from having sexual intercourse until two months after the delivery.

The observance of a special sacrifice to the spirits should be held between three months and a year after the child's birth, or it is held that the family will meet with certain disaster. This rite, performed as usual by the witch-doctor calls for a pig to be slaughtered as an offering to the spirits. The pig must be at least two months old. While some rites - such as the blessing of the baby and the offering to the spirits - can be undertaken by an ordinary witch-doctor *sai ton* (moh phi lek - "small" witch-doctor), there are cases that require the presence of the *toom sai kong* (moh phi yai "big" witch-doctor). This is when the child birth seems likely to be complicated.

There are special rules to be observed even in inviting *toom sai kong!* The man who goes to fetch this type of witch-doctor must arrive back at the house where the expectant mother is alone, shutting the door behind him but leaving it unbolted. When the witch–doctor arrives he has to kick the door open himself. Unlike ordinary witch–doctors who wear ordinary clothes, the senior witch–doctor is dressed in special garments to indicate his rank. He has a *kim* (a dagger–like knife), a water–buffalo horn, a bell and a pair of bamboo clacking sticks. Arriving at the house, he kicks open the door and strides towards the expectant mother.

He then consults his treatise on child birth. There are three stages to be observed. The first calls for the illustration of a man pulling the hands of a child. This is done on a piece of paper which is burned after the drawing is completed. The witch–doctor then mixes the ashes in a cup of water while chanting sacred utterances specified in the text. The cup is given to the woman to drink to help facilitate easy delivery. The final stage is the most exciting. Before giving the sacred water to the woman, he dips his dagger into the solution. Suddenly he pretends to scrape her stomach. He does this repeatedly whilst uttering weird incantations. At intervals he rings the bell, blows on the horn, sounds the clacking sticks and dances around. His gait and attitude are supposed to seem threatening both to the woman and to the unborn child. All these efforts are intended to induce a safe delivery. However, without the woman's co–operation they become futile.

'Farm-ching' - the 16 spirits. These paintings of the spirits are passed from generation to generation. The dance honouring 'Farm-ching' takes place every three years.

Sickness

The senior witch-doctor is also responsible for special ceremonies such as the *pienhoong* (paying

Reed boats laden with bundles representing evil spirits. The Yao will float these boats down stream from the village in an act of cleansing it.

Examples of some of the different types of scales used both by the witch-doctor and in daily life.

The witch-doctor at another of his tasks – blowing 'holy' water onto the seeds of the next season's grain crop to make for a more bountiful harvest.

The weight of the seeds is judged by the witch-doctor. Heavy means a good crop, light fortells bad luck.

respect to the great spirits) or the renewal of life rite which is intended to lengthen the life of a person close to death.

The Yao also rely on witchcraft in cases of serious illness. To improve the condition of the sick person, the senior witch–doctor writes the patient's name on a piece of paper and then tries to stick the paper onto pictures of the *pienhoong* – the 18 Great Spirits. Whichever spirit the paper sticks to, is considered the one that will consent to adopt the sick person as it's son - and the "adopted son" soon recovers! Because the *pienhoong* picture is rare, the owner often entrusts it to another family. Every year there is a big ceremony to pay homage to the *pienhoong*.

In dealing with illnesses, second and third stages are evoked only when the first fails. The methods are the same – only the illustrations and incantations differ. The picture in the second stage is of a man fighting a heron while another man tries to snatch a baby from a fish's mouth. The third illustration depicts a man being attacked by two large birds.

In cases of mild illness, Yao use methods such as changing the name of the person to that of an animal. If the sick person is a child, a senior person in the village may be found to adopt it, after which it continues to live with its natural parents.

Death

The death of a Yao is observed by lying the body in state on a raised stretcher for from three to five days if he was a rich person or for one day if he was poor. There is a bathing ceremony after which the body is placed in a coffin for burial or cremation. Lamps or torches are lit at the head and feet during the lying in state. The ceremony is held in the house if the person dies there. If the

A Yao opium farmer busy collecting the juice from the poppy harvest.

person dies outdoors, the ceremony is held in the open air.

Yao hold that a place for burial or cremation must be well away from the house or the village. If this is not followed, disaster and ruin would follow.

After the body is placed in the coffin, it is carried in procession to the burial site. The people are led as usual by a witch-doctor. In this instance he waves a bunch of special grass to ward off evil spirits. The witch-doctor is the only person who can perform a cremation ceremony. Before lighting the pyre, he walks around the coffin twice and over it once while relatives and friends of the dead person put wood on the pyre. When sufficient wood is in place, the witch-doctor opens the coffin lid with his foot and walks around the coffin from three to seven times. He then kneels to light a fire on a bamboo tray in front of him, turning his back to the coffin. After the tray is well alight, he throws it over his shoulder onto the pyre without turning to look at the coffin.

In selecting the place for burial or cremation, the witch-doctor tosses a hen's egg into the air and lets it fall. Where the egg breaks is the selected site.

The collection of ashes is undertaken three days after the cremation. Again an egg is used for choosing the burial site. A hole is dug where the egg breaks and the ashes are buried there.

Thus, the life cycle - birth, marriage, health, sickness and eventual death - goes on uninterrupted in the traditional fashion of the Yao........

Left: Poppy harvesters design and make their own knives to extract the opium juice. They may be two or three bladed. In Yao it is called 'in-yu-bai'.

Below: The Yaos' agricultural implements (l. to r.) digging stick 'jem-joey,', curve-edged knives 'hyu-ngao' and hoe 'tua-sor'.

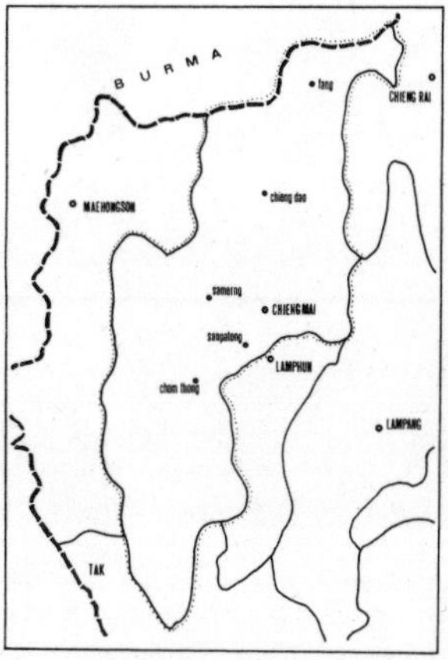

Total of villages :	*148*
Total of households :	*4,743*
Total population :	*37,477*

MIAO

Some scholars today contend that the Miao hill tribe is, in fact, a section of Yao and have no separate identity as such. However, it will be seen that although there are obvious similiarities between the way of living of Miao and Yao in their settlements in Northern Thailand, they form a distinct group with many facets of their life very different from their Yao neighbours.

As with Yao, Miao have physical characteristics similar to the Chinese. When the tribes filtered south, the Miao which entered Thailand composed three groups : Black Miao or Blue Miao (Mong Yua), White Miao (Mong Doe) and Striped Miao (Mong Kor Paan). The Miao do not associate with

Some Miao returning from market.

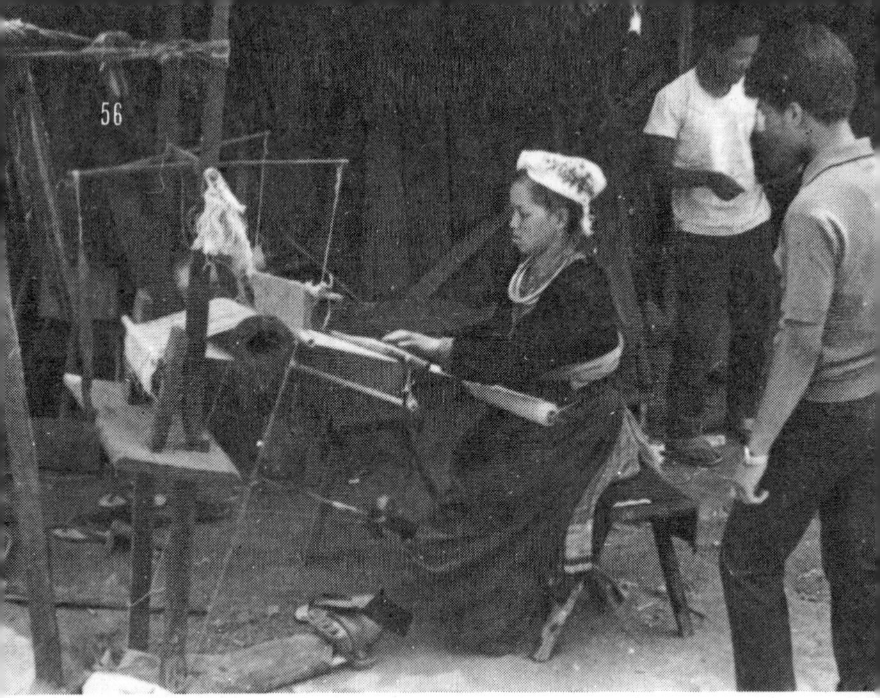

A Miao woman weaving clothing for hereself and her family.

other tribes, although the three "colour" groups speak the same language and generally get along even if they do not share the same village. The colour distinction is a curiosity as it refers only to their costumes and its origin is unknown.

Although exact figures are not known, their total number in Thailand (excluding refugees from Laos) is more than 37,000. The majority have settled along the border with Laos, mainly in Chiang Rai, Prae, Lampang, Mae Hong Son, Chiang Mai.

They prefer, like Yao, to live on hills at least 3,000 to 4,000 feet above sea level. As will be seen, their livelihood is often associated with the opium poppy and much effort is being made to get them to adapt to other crops.

A Miao youth carving a vessel for holding pig swill.

A Miao's larder is under the roof. Seen hanging may be maize, gourds, chillis and seeds for the next crop planting season.

Housing

The houses of the Miao are similar to those of Yao and Lisu in that they use the hard ground for their floor while they sleep on raised platforms, about a foot above the ground. The floors for sleeping are of split bamboo. Elephant grass, palm leaves, split bamboo or whatever else is available in the area of the village is used for roofing and it nearly touches the ground outside the house.

The village visited was Huay Mae Choe, which straddles the Thai/Burmese border - but this distinction is not meaningful to villagers. The Miao in this village do not travel far although some of the men would like to seek marriage partners from distant villages - there is a shortage of

A young girl looks after her baby brother whilst the parents are busy in the fields.

Miao women wear pants covered with white pleated skirts. On this festive occasion a group are seen with silver neck rings and on their heads silver chains with delicate designs of birds and fish.

potential brides in this village. The villagers feel safe enough to travel to the important nearby market at Mae Sa-long, and trade with Hors or Chinese troops (KMT 93rd. Division) who do not harass them when relations and trade are cordial. At the market, Miao can buy or see the artifacts

Above: Miao women keep their hair short at the back and sides. On top it is left long and swept into a knot. In hot weather they will wear a turban to protect themselvs from the heat.
Below: Young Miaos (and an oldster) are not shy of the camera.

A young Miao girl carrying bamboo joints to fetch water from the well at the base of the hill.

A young boy returns from collecting fire wood. Miao children help in the household chores from about the age of five.

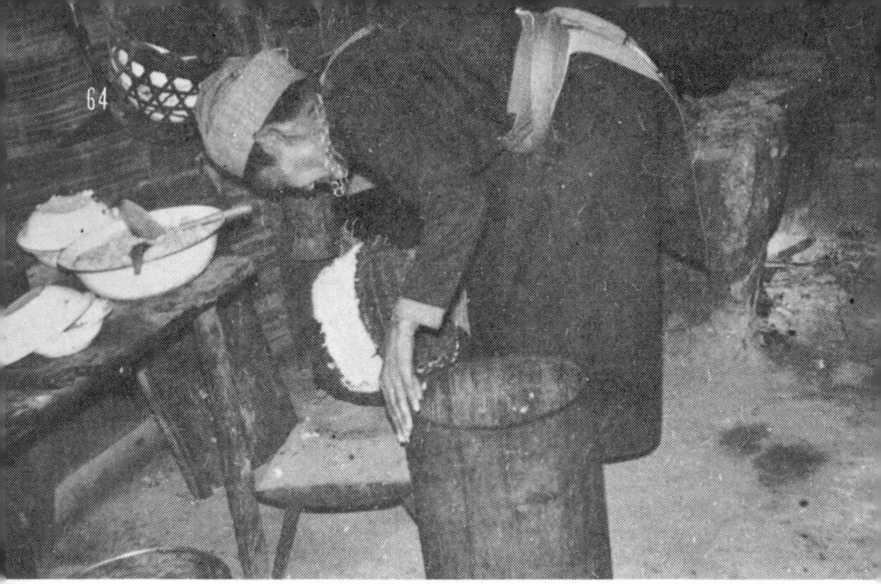

A Miao woman cooking for family and visitors.

of a strange civilization with which they have no other contact.

Place of women

Women in Huay Mae Choe and other Miao and Yao villages visited seem to live a life of servitude. Women and children till the fields and hunt for animals in the jungle while the men can usually be found in their homes smoking opium. All pursuits of the men seem to be one form of recreation or another. Women do not even find solace in their language as there seems to be no words in Miao for "pity" or "show respect" to women.

Spirit worship

The spirits of the ancestors, the sky, the wind and the forest are all given due respect in the Miao household. In houses there are usually two shelves for the spirits. One is for the head of the house and is known as *dhat-jee-uar-neng,* and a second

Two altars can be seen in every Miao house. One is for ancestral worship, 'he second is for the spirit of the sky. Decorations are of paper or of cut bamboo shoots. Bamboo joints serve as cups.

A Miao woman kills a chicken as an offering to the spirit of the house which caused the sickness of her son.

for the eldest son and called *dha-tu-uar-neng.* The hilltribe peoples take their form of worship as seriously as do those of the usual religions and are greatly offended if it is suggested to them that their spirits exist only in their imagination.

Before going out to hunt, Miao will consult the spirits to determine whether it is an auspicious time or not. If the signs seem unfavourable, they will not go out but if they interpret them as good, then they will go out in search of prey. Their system is foolproof since when no mammals or birds are caught, frogs will serve to demonstrate the infallibility of the spirits! The hunter, usually a woman, will wear a scarf embellished with magic signs to ensure good fortune.

The traditional Chinese calendar is used to calculate the dates considered auspicious for important events such as weddings and other big ceremonies. Yao, being more literate and knowledgeable about chronology are sometimes consulted, but in some Miao villages those dealing with spirit matters have learned the calendar from their predecessors and obviated the need for inter-tribal consultation.

The treatment of illness in a Miao village involves flattering the shaman exorcist who has best contact with the spirits. When a member of a family is taken ill, the shaman will be called in to hear his ability praised. Other family members will laud his abilities as a man of medicine and seek his favour with an opium pipe. The head of the house will prepare bowl after bowl of opium for the exorcist and offer him tea to moisten his parched throat. An outside observer might be led to the conclusion that the witch-doctor was more concerned with the opium than the welfare of his patient. However, the sick person frequently sits

As New Year draws near, Miao women are seen grinding glutinous rice to make cakes.

Facing: Miao display their colourful costumes to advantage when taking part in the New Year celebrations.

up and talks or tries to talk cheerfully with the shaman. As little effective medical treatment is administered, this phenomena of "faith" curing probably does more good than harm.

Sexual Freedom

Young members of the tribe have complete sexual freedom. There is no stigma attached to a

Miao girl for being an unmarried mother. On the contrary, a child is seen as a girl's best proof that she is fertile. This complete sexual license gives young tribal people of both sexes the opportunity to gain considerable experience in the ways of the body.

Miao girls are neither shy nor coy and readily invite men of the same tribe to sleep with them. There seems to be no problems of jealousy. This early sexual spree for the young girl ends not with her becoming pregnant, as in most societies, but when a prospective husband makes a monetary offerings to the girl's parents - a similar situation to Yao sinsord. Typical offerings range from 100 to 400 silver rupees, which Miao use to decorate their costumes. They shun paper money and prefer to deal only in silver. The silver Indian rupees, minted in the days of the British Raj, are the closest to conventional currency in villages of Miao and other hill tribes.

Marriage

The wedding ceremony itself is more the occasion for a feast and is very lavish without being complicated. Relatives of the bride will slaughter pigs and fowl, and, if available, cattle. The number of people attending and the length of the wedding festivities are in proportion to the status of the bride's family. The village-brewed strong drink

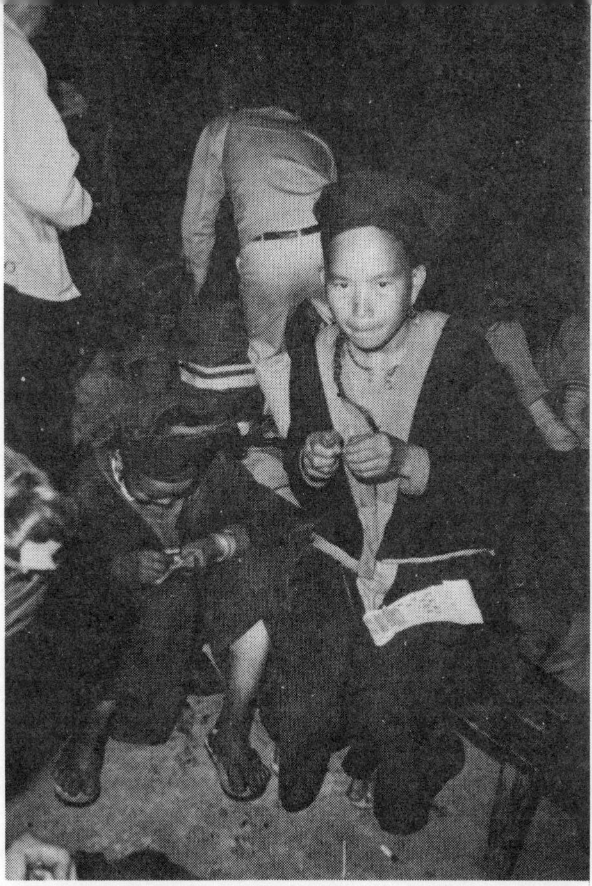

The women do not stop their intricate stitching even when strangers arrive in the village.

flows freely at the feast.

With the wedding over, the woman quickly settles down to her tasks of bearing children, carrying water, pounding rice, weaving cloth, working in the fields and harvesting both food crops and the

Miaos are very fond of making music. This man is playing a Chinese-type instrument called a 'kaen'. It has it's counterpart in Laos and other parts of North east Thailand.

Facing: Miao seen performing on the 'kaen' at an outdoor ceremony.

ubiquitous opium. If she has no sons or young boys to help her she has also, as mentioned earlier, to hunt as well. With these tasks completed, the woman is not entitled to rest. In the evenings she must knead opium and heat it for her husband's

A young Miao woman cutting the poppy to allow the opium juice to extrude in the form of a white gum. Harvesting is usually in March.

pipe. Her day is over when the man of the house dozes off into an oblivion of opium-induced dreams!

Food

Miao are not great gourmets and their food needs are simple. They are usually satisfied with rice and some meat or vegetables. They may eat pork, beef, wild or semi-domesticated fowl, monkeys and langurs. Whatever vegetables thrive in their particular area are used to provide some variety to the diet. These may be gourds, pumpkins, taro roots, sweet potatoes, bamboo shoots, maize and lettuce. Onions and coriander serve as spices. The liquor, such as that used in the wedding feast, is distilled by the villagers from maize, paddy or sometimes wheat.

When eating Miao prefer using chopsticks – another indication of their Chinese ancestry. Their rice is cooked in wooden jackets, but one sign of

A pedlar (right) exchanges his vermicelli for raw opium. Opium is often used as a means of currency.

their affluence is the growing use of aluminium rice pots.

Miao get their income for trading purposes from the cultivation of crops. Formerly it was only the opium poppy, but they are slowly being induced to turn to other crops and the raising of animals such as pigs, oxen, buffalo, cattle, goats and chickens. H.M. King Bumibol has taken a keen interest in helping the people of all tribes and was instrumental in introducing sheep and goat raising to the Miao and other tribes. The West German government gifted Merino sheep in this project.

Domesticated animals are under the care of the children. The animals are allowed to roam freely in field or forest during the day and the youngsters are sent out to bring them home when darkness falls.

In most hill tribe villages, sanitation is taken care of by scavanger dogs and pigs. To a visitor this way is, to say the least, disconcerting - but it does keep the area around the house clear of human and other waste.

Clothing

The clothing of Miao is basically black. Men and women both wear long black pants. The men cover the upper half of the body with short jackets, so short that they leave the navel exposed. Around their waist men tie red checkered cloth. On their heads they wear a round Chinese hat. The more fashion conscious of them prefer this to be made of felt.

Over their pants, the women wear a pleated skirt. Attached to the skirt is a dangling piece of beautifully embroidered cloth. They wear a piece of plain cloth around the waist and a low turban wrapped around the head. This forms the everyday wear of Miaos. For special events they adorn themselves with more elaborate attire and silver ornaments. The women's turbans are more elaborate and their skirts are woven in colourful embroidery. The jackets have green stripes around the sleeve ends and the necking. This continues down the front and around the lower hem. Around their waist women tie a band of red cloth.

During special occasions, they wear their turbans with a tilt to one side and featuring bright pieces of knitted yarn. The area from waist to calf is covered with a striking loin cloth, fully embroidered. On these occasions, too, the men try to outdo each other in silver jewellery. The man wearing the most rings is deemed the most desirable from a marital point of view and thus attracts the most attention from the unmarried girls. He also has a jacket trimmed with green striped cloth. Some men sport Mandarin hats, others black skull caps topped by coloured woollen baubles. A few wrap turbans around their heads.

Opium Cultivation

A study of the cultivation of opium by Miao is an essential part of understanding and appreciating the tribe's culture and way of life. It is also required knowledge for those who sincerely want to help these people to forsake the age-old practice and former economic basis of their lives.

Planting and tending the young plants takes place between August and November. In December, the opium poppy blossoms and bears seeds. The average time from the sprouting of the seed to the time of harvesting the raw opium is some three to four months. The harvesting season lasts from January to March. During this time the tribesmen build small shelters in their fields to ensure their protection during the critical harvesting time. A welcome visitor will find tribesmen sitting in their shelters conversing and smoking opium or local-grown tobacco whilst sheltering from the heat of the day or the chill of the night. Inside the shelter is a make-shift kitchen to prepare food and boil water for tea.

There are nine species of opium poppy of which the author has seen three. These had white, violet and whitish-orange flowers. Yields were said to be the same for each of these three types. At maturity an opium poppy plant will grow to a height of four to five feet, and if well tended will produce two harvests of raw opium.

At the time of writing, a Miao family cultivating opium can earn on the average 4,000 to 6,000 baht a year (US$200 to US$300). Less income is derived from livestock and very few at the present time cultivate vegetables for commercial purposes. As was earlier mentioned, great efforts are being made by various groups to induce the Miao to change to other crops.

Miao and other tribes pay a high price for growing opium as many become addicted to the drug and suffer poor health. Hard addicts are a frightening sight indeed being little more than skin and bones and incapable of taking any care of themselves.

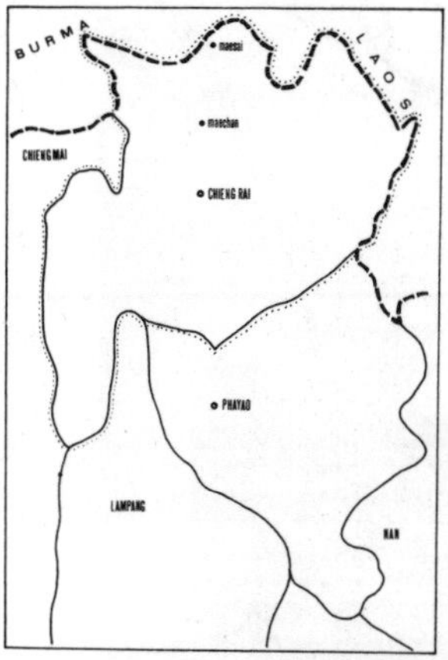

Total of villages :	*94*
Total of households :	*2,115*
Total population :	*13,566*

AKHA

In the northernmost Thai province of Chiang Rai visitors sometimes come across groups of hill tribes people dressed in strange attire walking with bamboo baskets hanging from their shoulders - and being followed by dogs. These people are the small tribe of Akha. They will have come down from their isolated villages high on the mountain shopes in Amphoe Mae Chan to barter or sell their goods, principally grass for brooms, cotton, tobacco and dried chillies - and to take back dogs with them. These dogs, however, are not destined to become household pets. They are for food, for Akha consider dog meat to be the tastiest available.

Without a trace of shyness, this Akha housewife pounds rice, bared to the waist.

This dog is not a pet - he is probably to morrow's dinner. Note the women carrying the heavy sacks of rice.

They migrated from China's Yunnan province to the Burmese Shan states before settling in the north of Thailand some sixty or seventy years ago. Most of their villages are small - usually from ten to forty houses - on remote slopes. Most hill tribes have settled on lower terrain, but the

An Akha woman adorned with solid silver necklaces and silver plates

An Akha woman working in the fields shades her head with a bamboo-plaited hat.

An Akha village set in the hills about 4,000 feet above sea level.

Akha chose to have their villages on higher ground to escape being disturbed by others.

They build their houses on watersheds with no ravines or other natural sources of water so they have to go down to lower valleys and carry water back up the hill for their daily needs. It is said that water flows to all the hill tribes with the exception of Akha who have to fetch their own.

Akha are very industrious people, but they rank as perhaps the poorest and most under-developed tribe in the country - and with probably the lowest standard of living. Among the tribes of Thailand they are considered at the bottom of the social scale.

Cotton is one crop every family grows. When there is a good harvest the surplus is sold to other tribes. It is on these selling trips that one may meet Akha. With some of the money they may visit Yao villages to buy or smoke opium. Many men are so addicted to it - and so poor - that they may even smoke the residue extracted from used pipes. Both men and women, like many older generation country Thais, chew betel to the extent that their teeth are greatly discoloured.

Both men and women keep their pipes with them. Smoking away, this young girl sets off to work. Tobacco is seen drying on the roof of the house.

Again bared to the waist, this women has her smoking pipe behind her ear.

Diet of Dogs

Dog meat is as important to Akha as pork or beef to other tribes. On trade routes they lead their dogs in packs, chained together by the owner. During the trip, they may slaughter one of the animals for a meal. The ear-splitting sound of

This married Akha woman is certainly not camera shy.

Below: The early morning is a busy time for the women. Here they are seen fetching the water for the day's use in the house.

This Akha girl has come down from the village on the hills for fishing.

An Akha woman using her bamboo fan to winnow paddy.

barking dogs usually accompanies any Akha journey. It's effect on the owners is probably only to whet the appetite!

Inflation has even crept into the dog market in recent years. The price of the meat has risen some sixteen fold in a matter of a few years - and seems destined to continue to rise.

The slaughter of a dog is quick. The hapless

No, she is not dancing. This Akha girl is, in fact, spinning cotton.

animal is tied with a string around its neck. While one man holds the string, another creeps up from behind wielding a large club. He strikes the dog a heavy blow on the skull and it quickly drops to the ground - without even a whimper. Akha hold that if the dog lets out even the slightest sound, the meat will loose much of its flavour. Thus only skilled people perform the kill.

Other food

While dog meat is their favourite dish, Akha also breed pigs, oxen and goats for meat for themselves and for market. They cultivate rice, maize, chillies and other vegetables as well as their main cotton crop.

They are expert hunters using catapults, crossbows, rifles and traps. They go for deer, wild boar, porcupines and civet or wild cat. They keep parakeets as decoys and use bamboo branches pasted with a sticky sap taken from trees to trap cicadas, a winged chirping insect, for food. Although they are not fastidious in their diet, most

A woman weaves cloth for the family's clothing.

The village gate to be seen in every Akha village. At the base of the posts are wooden effigies of men and women.

Tha-pa-mha - a rough wood carving assumed to have human shape. Akha hold that its the duty of both sexes to breed and thus maintain the human race.

Every Akha girl is skilled in needlework. This girl is seen stitching her own attire.

families subsist on diets with a low nutritional value. The poorest families eat nothing but rice with chillies and salt for weeks on end.

Spirit Worship

Like most hill tribes, Akha worship spirits, but their rituals are very different from those of other groups. At the entrance to their villages

The Akhas make much of their swing festival. Left, they are seen constructing the swing for the forthcoming ceremony. Centre, boys and girls play on the 'merry-go-round' at the site of the festivities. Right, the lover rocks the swing while the Akha girl goes higher and higher.

they erect an arch to the spirits. This is adorned with figures of birds, rats and other animals. Through the archway they make a path, flanked on both sides by fences of arrow-shaped poles or bamboo stakes, leading to the village gate. At

Gongs, guns and crackers herald in the New Year for the happy Akhas, but (below): These older women, dressed to kill, do not appear quite so amused.

Facing: An Akha mother and her child show both the colourful nature of their dress and the decorations used to enhance their appearance.

Besides holding water, bamboo joints made excellent musical instruments. Here a group of Akha women are using them whilst dancing and singing during the New Year festival.

the foot of the gate's poles are small carved wooden figures symbolizing the two sexes. Akha believe that these figures will rejuvinate their fertility and result in the everlasting reproduction of their race.

Beside every house is a miniature hut - an Akha spirit house. These can also be erected by a roadside, in forest or field. Unlike other tribes, they never place shrines in their houses. The outdoor shrines are mostly ramshackle and untidy.

Way of Life

Akha tend to be illiterate and indifferent to the outside world. According to one tribal legend, it once had its own alphabet. The story goes that this alphabet, which was inscribed on a buffalo hide, was stolen and eaten by a dog - since then they have had no written language.

They pay little attention to what is going on beyond the scope of their immediate task of subsisting. The average family needs a small plot of land, simple food and clothing, a primitive shelter and nothing more. But they are happy with the little they have and are free from the desires for change. They are calm, jovial, friendly and helpful. Always ready to lend a hand to strangers at any time, they treat them as members of their own family. Visitors have reported that Akha girls make good masseuses - offering their services free of charge!

Clothing

Akha women wear short black blouses and skirts made from dyed cotton cloth. The blouses are collarless and have long sleeves. Some women embroider their blouses, especially the ends of the sleeves and the bodices. They wear beads and solid silver necklaces and often have silver plates hanging from their necks. The necklaces indicate the financial status of the wearer. Sometimes they wear specially woven pieces of coloured cloth around their waist.

The men wear black pants and partly embroidered, round-necked, long sleeved black coats. Richer men frequently decorate their coats with buttons and silver coins around the edges, at the shoulders and the chest. They wear turbans

An Akha farmer at work in his fields.

From the type of head dress worn, one can see that the girl on the left is unmarried. Every girl is free to choose her own husband.

and are unshod. Some men have bracelets around the wrists.

The life of the women reaches a transition at the age of 12 when they change their head covering. Girls younger than 12 years old wear plain, peakless cotton caps. This type of attire, one of the most heavily adorned of all the hill tribes, is a cone-shaped bamboo frame reinforced

Akha boys spin tops while the girls look on

with rattan strips. It is ornamented, among other things, with pieces of silver, brightly coloured feathers, puffs, squirrels' tails, small pearl-like seeds of a wild grain, wild boar tusks and beetles with glossy emerald-hued wings.

An Akha woman also wears a long piece of cloth edged with a row of coins around her forehead. This must be put on before the ornate headdress. As the row of coins hang freely on the forehead, it appears to be part of the headdress. How richly decorated this head attire is depends on the taste and financial status of the woman.

Although close attention is paid to what is

worn on the head, the women, like the men, spend their lives bare foot. Most wear puttees, however, around the shins.

Instinctive sex

Sexual behaviour among Akha is free, dramatic and, it seems, instinctive. In the early evening, after the day's work and eating are over, young people get together at a meeting place especially arranged for them. They sing songs, giggle and dance, often in pairs. Some young men play a *naw,* a musical instrument made of flat

With a 'kaen' playing inviting music, the boys are ready for an evening's merry-making with the girls. An invitation to sex, in fact.

pieces of bamboo. Soon couples slip away and disappear behind bushes. Not long afterwards they will reappear, laughing and joking even more, and again join in the communal fun. Youngsters are free to have sexual intercourse as they please anywhere but in their houses - this is strictly taboo. Couples do not feel embarrassed by showing their affection for each other in front of strangers.

The affairs often - but not always - end in marriage. If a girl becomes pregnant she has to tell who her lover is. The man in question is then sought out to substantiate or disclaim her story. If he denies it, she becomes an evil omen to be

As men and women cannot eat together, this "hen" party was pictured at an Akha wedding ceremony.

The special Akha house where newly-weds may have intercourse. The family house has many sexual taboos!

expelled from the village as soon as possible and not to return until after the child is born. Even then she must build a new house for herself if she wants to live in that village again.

Marriage

Marriage for Akha means the setting up of a separate home, since the newly weds are not allowed to stay permanently with their parents. Every house will have a smaller hut built close to it which can accomodate two people. It is at the rear of the big house. This small hut is to be used by the newly married son and his wife whenever they want to have sexual intercourse - until their own house is built. This lovers' nest is built on long poles high above the ground so that it seems to roack in the wind. It is said that the higher it is the happier the couple will feel.

Housing taboos

Houses are made of the same materials as those of other tribes. However, Akha floors are well above the ground. Adjoining the floor of every house is an unroofed, raised platform used for drying chillies, tobacco and cotton during the day and for cottage industries, such as spinning cotton and weaving baskets at other times.

Like other tribes, they make their own utensils using materials from forest or field. They use gourds to make water pitchers and bowls and bamboo stumps to make smoking pipes. They only buy those things they cannot produce themselves, such as iron tools and plastics.

The interior of the house is divided into two parts - one for each sex. The inner part, including the back door, is for women and the outer part, including the front door, is for the men. The demarcation is strictly observed in most households and rarely does anyone violate the taboo of crossing the dividing line. But there is one exception. The husband can negotiate this frontier for the purpose of having intercourse with his

On H.M. the King of Thailand's birthday - December 5 - the Department of Public Welfare offer a special meal to all hill tribes people. Here Akla enjoy their meal.

wife. When his mission is completed he does not linger in the rear section of the house but quickly returns to the male half.

Each sex even has its own cooking stove since the common use of one is also taboo. These customs cause misunderstandings from time to time when visitors think that Akha are being unfriendly inside the house by keeping at a distance if they are of the opposite sex.

Doomed babies

Another Akha custom is that a wife who gives birth to a malformed baby must go into exile after first seeing that the new-born baby is killed. They hold that the malformed baby, which is considered to be less than human, would bring disaster to the entire village if it were reared. Only the death of the child can change the situation.

The mother must live in exile for three days, but before leaving the house she has to take off her usual clothing and adorn herself in nothing but leaves. She wanders around in this strange attire until she meets a well-wisher who will give her shelter and new clothes. Then, after returning to her village, she has to undergo purification rites before being permitted to live there again. These rites, undertaken by the woman in the presence of a witch-doctor,include changing her clothes again and herself slaughtering three pigs, three goats and three dogs.

The completion of this ceremony, however, does not give the woman full membership of the community again. She is not allowed to live in her former house but must build a new, small one at the far end of the village. She is not allowed to fetch water from the same spot as other villagers but must go down stream. She cannot even speak to other villagers and must make way for them whenever she meets them on a trail. Her husband suffers similarly.

Parents sometimes treat their children like pets, offering them - mostly the girls - for sale to other hill tribes for 500 baht to 1,000 baht (US$25 to US$50). Some sell their children because of poverty, which may be the result of debts incurred in buying opium on credit. The biggest buyers of Akha children are Yao. The children will later be given Yao names and treated as if they were Yao children. They are also allowed to use their Yao foster parents' surname.

Akhas are truthful and faithful people. They observe their taboos strictly even if they seem irrational at times. Examples include not allowing a wedding to be held until after a harvest; a pregnant woman cannot pass through the centre of a village. There is even a taboo on a husband and wife travelling together although a wife can travel with another man on a journey that may last several days and nights. But the husband need not worry - Akha do not commit adultery. A wife has only one husband, a husband has only one wife. They remain faithful to each other. In this respect, perhaps, they differ from most of the other diverse people in Thailand.

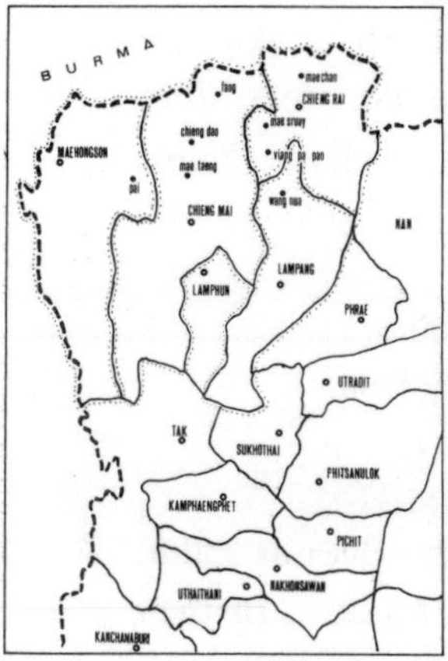

Total of villages : *179*
Total of households : *3,857*
Total population : *22,584*

LAHU

Of Thailand's many hill tribes, the Lahu - or Muser as the Thais call them - are perhaps the smallest group and thus among the least known. But they are so interesting that no study of the hill tribes can be made without at least a brief look at the Lahu history and way of living. They are an easy-going people who combine hard work with the ability to play and have created for themselves a life style to be envied in the troubled world of today.

Lahu, like most Thais, came from Yunnan province in south west China, and their appearance

A Lahu girl sets off for the fields.

in northern Thailand took place about the turn of this century. Of Tibeto-Burman stock, they came south in search of more fertile land. Those presently living in Thailand can be divided into four groupings :

(a) Lahu Nyi (Muser Daeng)

(b) Lahu Na (Muser Meung Nua)

(c) Lahu Shi (Muser Luang)

(d) Lahu Shehleh (Muser Dum)

All groupings refer to themselves as Lahu, but Thais and Shan call them Musur. In their previous homeland - China - they are called Lo Hei.

A bevy of Lahu Shehleh (Muser Dum) girls dressed in their native attire.

Lahu Nyi

The Lahu Nyi prefer to live on slopes high in the hills. They have established their villages in very rugged terrain in the Thai provinces of Chiang Rai, Mae Hong Son, Chiang Mai and in one part of Lampang. Usually their villages are smaller than those of any other tribe - some have only five or six houses and the normal is no more than 10 to 15. Lahu Nyi use the ubiquitous bamboo for their houses which are single room structures with six to nine wooden poles supporting the walls and roof. They normally measure 12 to 18 feet by 9 to 12 feet. They use thatch or palm leaves for roofing to keep out the rain.

The hearth is built in the middle of the room and serves as the main cooking area as well as a source of warmth in the colder winter months. The rest of the room serves both as storehouse and sleeping quarters. Guests are also received and entertained in this one room.

Lahu Nyi tribal costume worn by women is made of black cloth marked with broad stripes of red, white and blue around the collar, breast, hems and sleeves of the loose jacket and skirt.

Lahu Na

Lahu Na - Muser Meung Nua - are thus named because of the black tribal costume worn by the men. Women are likewise dressed but add

A young couple of Lahu Na, looking very smart in their special clothes.

narrow white strips of cloth on their dresses here and there as decoration.

Their houses are also made of bamboo but are somewhat larger than those of the Lahu Nyi. The majority of Lahu Na live in the Fang and Mae Taeng districts of Chiang Mai. There are also a few scattered villages in Mae Hong Son and Tak provinces. Chow Oie, a typical village in Fang, has some 45 houses with a total population of about 400 people.

The men are very skilled at fashioning bamboo into furniture and utensils and farm tools. In addition they are adept iron and silversmiths, good hunters and experienced farmers. Rice is grown, maize, a few vegetables and, of course, opium poppies. The women excel in needlework and weave their own cloth. Each girl is expected to make not only her own wedding dress but also the costume of her future husband.

Outdoor work begins at an early hour. Couples, with their young children carried on their

The average Lahu house is very shabby, small and dirty.

backs, first pound the rice singing as they do so. The sound of the work and music floods the landscape. Not adverse to hard work, a Lahu Na woman can often be seen walking along breast feeding a baby, a basketful of vegetables or firewood strapped on her back and a bamboo tray of rice balanced on her head. Bamboo containers are used to fetch water from nearby streams. With breakfast ready, the family will sit around the hearth for a very simple meal of rice garnished with salt and chillis.

Meat, be it beef, chicken or pork, is considered a delicacy and even simple vegetable soup with rice and the meat of birds is eaten only on special occasions. After breakfast, the domestic animals are fed. Chicken and pigs are raised to serve as offerings to the gods or the spirits of ancestors more than to be eaten or sold in distant markets. Every village girl is expected to care for a special pig which will eventually be slaughtered for her wedding day feast.

When the morning sun is high, the men load up their pack horses and take to the fields to tend the crops for the day, returning in the early evening. The women are by no means idle. They have to look after the children and the house or they may in season be cutting grass or sowing seeds in fields often a mile or two from home. If the wife is busy and there is no work to be done in the fields, the men take over the task of looking after the children.

A Lahu family busy with their handicrafts.

A Lahu woman returning from the fields laden with paddy sacks.

This is, of course, in direct contrast to Miao and Yao who, it has been seen, leave most chores to the women.

Lahu Na people are very ford of music and like nothing better than to sing and dance. Frequent festivals in honour of the great spirit *Uesah* are held in the evenings in a fenced off area which serves as a dance floor.

If a member of the family falls sick, the head of the house will slaughter a large pig as an offering to the gods. In addition he will donate a stepping plank to the village. This board will be placed about 100 yards from the entrance to the village. After he donation, villagers will dance and play an instrument called *kaen* to lure back the sick person's spirits which are thought to have gone wandering. The music is said to tempt the

During the New Year festivities, Lahu men and women dance round the sacrificial site day and night.

A Lahu Na girl feeding her own pigs which will later be slaughtered and offered to the spirits.

spirits to join them in their dancing and then to return to their owner.

If there is a visitor in the village, he will be asked to tie a thread around the wrist of the sick person as it is believed that visitors are the bearers of good luck. After the string tying ceremony, the visitor will be invited to join in the dancing and music making. In the centre of the dancing area a large bonfire is built and set alight. Villagers, regardless of age or sex, will join in the festivities which can last until the early hours.

Every New Year a bamboo archway is erected

and blessed by the *Poo Chong,* about whom more later. Each villager will pass under the archway in the understanding that by so doing they will, through the power of their respective spirits, avert any catastrophe. With the completion of this ceremony, the woven bamboo of the archway is taken down and thrown away.

Lahu Shi

The Lahu Shi reside in one village in Amphoe Muang, Chiang Mai, and in three other villages in Amphoe Mae Chan in Chiang Rai province. There is a total of about 100 houses and some 400 to 500 inhabitants in these three latter

A Lahu Nyi girl.

villages. They speak a dialect very similar to the other Lahu.

The men wear black coats, skirts and trousers with white and red hems. This they are gradually discarding in favour of the dress of other Lahu, It is thus becoming difficult to distinguish this particular small group. For the women, the normal daily wear resembles that of the Lahu Nyi. They wear long black dresses with red bands at the waist and sleeve ends. The head gear is black and white. For special occasions there is a special attire, resembling that of Lisu except for differences in the ornamentation.

A Lahu man praying to the spirits to protect his family and animals from sickness.

Lahu Shi celebrate their New Year twice. The major event - which comes first - is for the women and lasts for three days. The second, following closely on the first, is only for the men of the village. On both occasions each family will make a traditional offering of a pig to the spirits. A pole is erected in the centre of the village and a stall set up nearly. Pork and cakes of pounded, unsweetened glutinous rice are displayed on the stall. Day and night during the festivals, people of both sexes dance around the pole. There is also pouring of water to seek the forgiveness of their ancestors.

Young men and women will often make trips to distant villages at this festive time. They will be received by villagers of their own age group who will act as hosts. Together they feast, dance and sign and occasionally sneak off into the bushes to enjoy sexual intercourse.

Speaking of sexual matters, every Lahu Shi village has a pavilion where a young man can sit and await for the girl of his choice. When he wants a girl to leave her house and go to him in the pavilion, he will use a leaf to blow a signal - or even sing softly to her. When she hears his signal - and is agreeable to the tryst - she will answer him in song and run to join him.

The young couple then walk hand in hand to the pavilion. There he will plead his case and

Paradise: When a courtship proves successful, it is to a place like this that the young Lahū man will lead his fiancée to consumate their agreement.

if she is willing he will lead her into the nearby bushes to consumate the agreement.

Once this pre-marital intercourse is over, the girl will tell her parents what has taken place. The parents then discuss the matter with the head-man. If the young man admits to the act, no fee is asked of him except a chicken which he presents to the girl's parents. Thus the stage is set for a celebratory feast. No further ceremony is required to mark the fact that the two youngsters are now man and wife. The new groom moves into his bride's house to live for two years - or for as long as has been agreed upon by the man and the girl's parents.

The Lahu Exorcist

Every Lahu village has its own *Poo Chong* or exorcist who acts on behalf of the gods and spirits to aid the villagers. He provides amulets against harm, presides over rituals and acts as spiritual counsellor to the sick. He will advise them to sacrifice chickens or pigs to invoke the blessings of the spirits of their ancestors or to appease the village or jungle spirits. As can be imagined, *Poo Chong* holds an exalted position in the village and is honoured both in times of plenty and in times of need.

His house serves as the village temple, a hospital as well as being a meeting hall. At the back of the house stands a pole for the centipede flag which is hoisted as a sign of homage both to gods and spirits. This flag is known as a *Thong Chae*. Every seven days, *Poo chong* burns beeswax candles and joss sticks and places offerings to the spirits at the base of the *Thong Chae*.

Confusion over Names

Lahu do not have family or surnames like Miao, Yao and Lisu. It is thus a difficult task to locate people unless one is very familiar with his or her personal history or ancestry. Equal confusion is created in that Lahu name their villages after the headman of the time. For a visitor this situation can be very confusing indeed - if the old headman has died since a previous visit. When such a death occurs, the village will take the name of his successor although it is known for a village to retain the name of a particularly illustrious late headman. The villagers honour him by declaring his name to identify the village in perpetuity.

Chilli Kings

Lahu are popularly recognised by Thai merchants as kings of the dried chillis - for this is their main trading item. They frequently meet with travelling Thai traders on grassy hilltops to exchange their chillis for sweets and other delicacies from the outside world. Other than this brief contact - and with occasional visitors to their village - Lahu seem to prefer to live on their own in quiet, deep hills, far from noise and confusion. They work hard, play hard and smoke their opium. Would "progress" bring them greater happiness? This is a moot question...........

Dried chillies being weighed prior to a visit to the market.

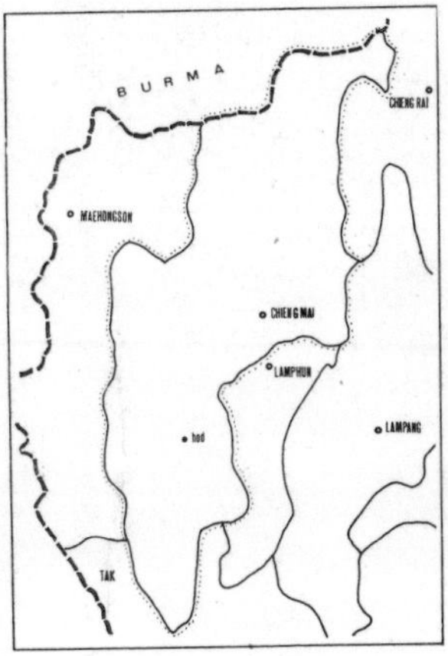

Total of villages :	*42*
Total of households :	*1,986*
Total population :	*11,250*

LAWA

Lawa belong to the Mon-Khmer ethic grouping. After clashing with the Khom and Thai, they were finally vanquished, moving into the forests and mountains of northern Thailand in about 1845 as well as parts of Burma and the frontier region of China's Yunnan province.

The majority of those now inhabiting Thailand are to be found in Amphoe Mae Sariang, Mae Hong Son province and in Amphoe Hot, Chiang Mai province. Ban Bor Luang is one of their largest villages and is on the main highway from Hot to Mae Sariang. Most Lawa people were born in their present villages, although some

A Lawa girl in traditional dress and decorations, enjoys a smoke.

A Lawa girl weaving. Lawa cloth is exceptionally beautiful.

wives have come from nearly villages. Many Lawa men have inter-married with women from the Karen hill tribe or Northern Thais.

Lawa have a history of consolidation of their villages. Some of the land formerly controlled by them in scattered villages has been taken over by Karen who moved into this region after the Lawa consolidated their settlements.

The Household

The basic unit of Lawa social structure is the household. The ideal is composed of husband, wife, their unmarried children and perhaps a married son and his wife and children. After a wedding, the bride and groom are supposed to live in the groom's house or that of his father. This does not always come about however. About a third of the married couples in a typical Lawa village were found to live in the house of the bride or her father.

Children are affiliated with the descent group of the household they live in. Thus a child will normally be a member of his father's descent group and will honour the spirit of his father's ancestors. When children are raised in the household of the wife's father, they will honour the spirit of his ancestors.

Ideally, the youngest son, when he gets married, should remain in his parents' household, caring for them in their old age. Two married brothers will rarely live in the same house for more than a few years. The elder Lawa brother will move out when the house becomes crowded with children and when he can afford to build a new one. As soon as he has his own house, the elder brother occupies a position in the descent group senior to both his younger brother and his father.

Irrigated fields belonging to a household are not usually divided after one brother sets up a new house. Instead they may be farmed in alternate years by the now two households or they may be farmed jointly and the proceeds split.

Love and Marriage

Young Lawa men do their courting according to old traditions. The youth plays the harp as he walks along the village street after dark, singing a love song. The Burman follows the same custom. When he arrives at the girl's house he creeps under the house where she is sleeping, sliding his hand through a chink in the floor boards to waken her. If the girl consents to this "proposal", she will come down and meet him immediately. The youth will take her to his kinsmen's house where she will stay for a few days.

The next step is the formal engagement. The young man will send a personal messenger to inform the girl's parents that he intends to marry her. The following day an engagement gift of a pig is sent to her parents. This will be slaughtered for a feast among her parents and their relatives. In the afternoon of the same day, the prospective son-in-law brings an engagement fee of between nine and 23 rupees, depending on agreement, to the parents.

At the time of the wedding, young women will prepare paddy for rice and unmarried male friends of the groom will lend a hand in fishing and cutting firewood for cooking many delicious dishes. Others have to build a joss-house to act as a banquet hall for the spirits.

In the evening a procession of bridesmaids escort the bride to the groom's house. The cere-

A man using a traditional means for shredding home grown tobacco.

monies for a well-to-do couple will last for two to three days and several pigs and chickens will have been slaughtered for the feast.

Marriage is generally for life. Divorce is disapproved of, and thus very rare and polygamy

Terraced rice fields in a Lawa upland farm. The most is made of badly irrigated land.

is not permitted. Remarriage of a widow or widower is, however, acceptable. Premarital and extra-marital intercourse is forbidden and is thought seldom to occur. Many Lawa women are known to be pregnant at the time of their wedding and an offering to the spirits which may have been offended by premarital intercourse is a regular part of all Lawa wedding ceremonies.

Marriage between couples belonging to the same descent group is forbidden. In a small village, where the number of available mates is limited, the structure of lineage groups may be altered by a decision of the elders of that lineage. In these cases, individuals whose closest common ancestor is more than three generations removed may marry. In addition to regulating marriage and co-operating in various tasks, the descent

A Lawa farm house at the side of the fields. Such a house is in constant use around harvest time.

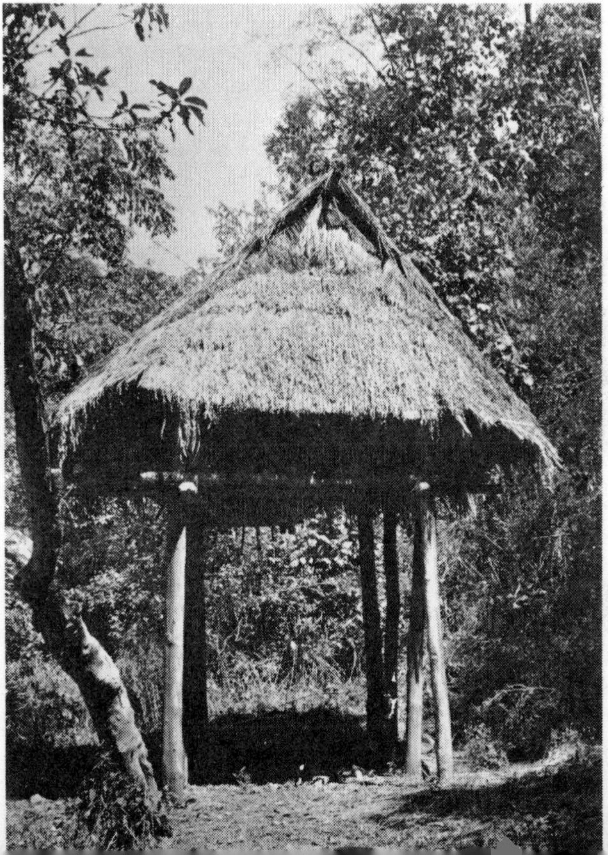

group are also ritual groups for certain ceremonies. In these, which concern the guardian spirits of the houses, each household in the descent group performs the ceremony aided by members of the others.

Ritual Leader

Each village should have a ritual leader and an assistant who are respectively the village elder and one born into that particular descent group.

Several *lams* (a slave lineage) together with other elders and with *smang* (a princely lineage) make up an informal council which discusses and

The hand-made Lawa wooden mortar which can be seen in every house.

Bamboo joints stacked in a Lawa House ready for the collection of water.

decides on issues of community-wide importance. These include violations of local customs and plans for communal agricultural activities.

The *smang* lineage exists in several Lawa villages; members claim descent from a princely lineage of the tribe and are accorded high prestige. This is reflected in the right to collect a higher than usual dowry and certain other rights. In the villages where they live, the senior male of the *smang* lineage is considered to be the chief religious officiant. He is the arbiter in questions appertaining to Lawa custom and tradition. He receives a small ritual payment from every couple getting married in the village. To protect his ritual know-

As with some other tribes, the Lawa hang a woven bamboo motif in front of the house of a sick person to ward off evil spirits.

ledge he must not attend funerals, but must compensate the bereaved family by making a token payment to them.

Administration

As in other villages under the central Thai administrative system, the headman of the Lawa is chosen by the villagers. This choice is approved and confirmed by district officers. This Lawa headman draws a small monthly salary with the obligations of attending monthly meetings at the district office (amphoe), of recording and reporting changes of residence, of assisting in the collection of taxes, of acting as the government spokesman in the village and of acting as host to official visitors etc.

Each Lawa village is well organized to perform the necessary community tasks by assigning equal responsibility to each household. This organization is reinforced by a system of taxation which, in effect, rewards those who contribute most to community activities and fines those who contribute the least. At the end of each year, following the ritual sacrifice to the village guardian spirit, the male heads of all households meet and discuss expenses incurred in the preceeding year. All expenses are counted : transporting guests, feeding official visitors, fighting forest fires etc.

Each household is obliged to send at least one man to help fight a fire. Credit for one day is given if more than one man goes from a particular household and a debit of one day against any household failing to send a man. Similar credits and debits are attached to other community projects such as clearing trails to upland fields, clearing a firebreak around fields before they are burnt. Likewise, a man will receive credit if he spends a day on village business. Expenses are totalled for the year and each household is assessed an equal amount. Those who have contributed less than the equivalent of this amount must pay taxes and those who have contributed more than their share in food and/or labour receive their balance due.

Law and Order

Violations of Lawa customs regarding property, bodily assault, marriage or sexual behaviour appear to be rare. There are occasional complaints about vegetable, rice or chicken thefts but no one is named as the culprit. The loss is usually blamed on outsiders. Disputes over rights to cultivate certain plots or grazing land are very common among the Lawa, but these are usually settled between the two parties before they are referred to the *smang.* Violations of customs concerning pre-marital intercourse are probably the most common. The matter becomes a problem only if the girl has become pregnant, in which case the solution is marriage.

Violation of incest taboos is a much more serious offence since it is held that a marriage in violation of these taboos will result in the creation of a malevolent spirit *(phee-ka)* which will enter and consume the inner organs of innocent bystanders. The cure for this is to drive the offenders from the village.

Illnesses and Cure

Most illnesses are diagnosed and treated by those who have studied the subject or are able to

Lawa are rarely without their pipes. Here two girls are enjoying a smoke.

Posts in a Lawa graveyard on which rest plates for offerings to the spirits.

communicate with spirits as a result of spirit possession. Although Lawa are familiar with a large number of herbal remedies, the most common form of treatment is by diagnosis through divination, using rice grains, rice liquor or chicken bones. The purpose of divination is to learn the name of the spirit believed to be causing the sickness and to learn the proper blood sacrifice that will satisfy that spirit. The spirit doctor determines the name of the spirit, addresses it by name and pledges the required animals. If he is lucky, the patient may show signs of recovery. If the patient gets no better or becomes worse, it is assumed that the divination has failed and the process is repeated until the patient recovers - or dies. Then it is assumed that the methods of detecting the spirit have been incorrect.

Several techniques of curing exist, including the use of incantations *(khar-tha)* or blowing on the patient's head or body. So *khar-tha* practitioners may be admired, or feared depending on the direction to which they turn their knowledge. The *khar-tha* came originally from the Indian tradition and are recorded in Burmese, Thai or Shan books, but Lawa, most of whom are illiterate, learn them by word of mouth and are unfamiliar with their origin.

Religion

Like most hill tribes, the traditional religion of Lawa is animism. The people derive their beliefs concerning spirits from a number of sources and hold that spirits dwell in all parts of the environment : houses, fields and forest, cemetery, sky, streams and rivers. They believe that these spirits can cause illness and must be fed. Other spirits influence the success of crops and still others can protect a household or the village from external harm.

As part of their animism, Lawa hold that if a woman dies in the child birth of a deformed child or one of evil appearance, the new-born baby should be buried with the dead mother. If the mother lives, as with Akha, the baby should be killed anyway because such a baby is thought to be a devil, not an ordinary human being, and if allowed to live in the village he or she will bring disaster to the whole community. Several children have been saved from such a fate and are now being cared for by foster parents.

Technology and the Economy

Lawa technology is based on a limited number of iron or manufactured tools. All households in the village are directly dependent on agriculture for their living. Those tools that cannot be made in the village have to be bought in the market.

Rice is the principal crop in both upland and irrigated fields. Upland fields are cleared from mid-January and cut trees and bushes allowed to dry until late March. Usually all the fields of a Lawa village lie in the same area and all are burnt at the same time on a day deemed auspicious by the *smang*. After burning, a few root crops are planted and unburnt logs and gathered, piled and burnt as quickly as possible so that planting may be completed before the beginning of the monsoon rains - which may be as early as May.

No fertilizer is used except ash from the burnt forest cover in the upland fields, and ash from burnt rice stubble in the irrigated fields. No consistent attempt is made to enrich the ground

Above: Close-up of a hand-carved Lawa boundary post. Right: In the foreground, a Lawa boundary post. Behind, some houses in a Lawa village.

by pasturing domestic animals on them, although Lawa are familiar with the effects of fertilizer and gather chicken and pig manure for use in their vegetable gardens.

Small handfuls of rice seed are thrown into shallow holes. The seeds are covered by the natural movement of the soil, which has become loose and friable following the burning. When the seedlings are about six inches high and the rain is falling regularly, they may be thinned out where they have been planted too thickly and transplanted into areas lacking in seed growth. Maize and mustard greens *(phak-kard)* are the first vegetables to ripen, starting in June. The rice harvest starts early in October and continues until late November.

After harvesting, upland fields lay fallow for nine years before being cultivated again. Irrigated rice cultivation starts with the preparation of rice nurseries, the repair of ditches and dams in late May or early June. When the fields have become rain soaked and softened, they are ploughed and harrowed and the seedlings are transplanted in July. The harvest usually ends late in October.

Every Lawa household has a winter garden in easily watered land alongside permanent streams. Work on these gardens starts in December, almost as soon as the harvested rice has been carried back to the village. These gardens provide much needed vegetable supplements by mid - January or February and continue to yield produce into April or May.

Most households own or share in the ownership of a variety of fruit trees such as pomelo, lime, jackfruit, mango, guava, betel, coconut etc. The age of a particular village can be deduced from the size of the jackfruit trees.

Lawa build their houses on piles, with a floor level some four or five feet above the ground. Walls and floors of wooden planks are popular

An old Lawa woman spins cotton which will later be used on a hand loom.

Cotton balls, which will each be dyed a different colour, will later trim the Lawa clothes.

among more prosperous families, while the others have walls of split or woven bamboo and flooring of split bamboo. Chicken and pigs are penned under the houses and firewood, ready for use, is stored in a special place under the house. The houses are roofed with shingles, thatch grass or palm leaves.

The women spin and weave cotton clothing, using cotton they have themselves grown in upland fields. They weave cloth on back-strap looms and blankets on back-strap or frame looms. Some items of men's clothing, especially trousers, have to be purchased and some men have home-spun shirts tailored as used by northern Thais.

Land Ownership

About 70 years ago, Lawa were considered to be subjects of the northern Thai princes. They

A Lawa woman chopping firewood using a home-made axe.

A typical spirit house. Egg, uncooked rice or a gourd is placed inside the house as an offering.

paid an annual tribute to the Prince of Chiang Mai or the Prince of Lamphun. In return they received grants from the princes, inscribed on silver sheets, confirming the Lawa right to land and to govern themselves. Grants of these types are not recognized by the Bangkok government and have no legal standing today. According to present Thai law, the hill lands are the property of the Crown.

As population increases and control of land is lost to outsiders - Karen from other villages - the pressure on land is the major problem of the Lawa. There is continual conflict between Lawa and Karen and annual encroachment on Lawa land is common. Lawa are at a disadvantage in this struggle because of their feeling about "togetherness". Karen have no hesitation making a field in the midst of Lawa fields, but Lawa feel much more secure if their upland fields are bounded on all sides by other Lawa fields.

Trade

Trade brings members of each family from a remote village down the valley at least once a

Some of the hand- made earthenware pots used in a Lawa house.

year. Trade is usually on a cash basis. Credit is seldom sought or received. The most common items traded are rice, usually milled, and pigs. Convenience seems to determine the choice of market merchant. Purchases are made from those merchants with whom there has been a long-time familiarity.

One item that the Lawa are turning to more is modern medicine. As has already been seen, traditional medicine - both herbal remedies and sacrifices to spirits - is a very important concern of and expense to Lawa. Shop-bought medicines are expensive and the search for medical care - both traditional and modern - is one of the more important reasons for contact with people outside the village.

Traditional medicine often requires consultations with spirit specialists from other Lawa or even Karen villages. Modern medicines are obtained from missionary doctors, or Thai government health officials or border police. All villagers recognise that modern medicine as more effective and usually cheaper than traditional medicine in the long run.

Lawa, like other hill tribes, have a feeling of respect towards the outside world but still like the company of their own kind. Every adult man and most women know some Northern Thai language as well as Karen and their own language. Children and adolescents are keen to learn and

The graveyard is littered with the possessions of the departed. No attempt is made to tidy the site.

speak both Northern Thai and Bangkok Thai and commonly use these languages to joke with one another

They accept the fact that they live in Thailand and expect Thai influence to increase in the future. They know that many of their relatives have gone to the lowlands to live and that moving to these lowlands implies "becoming Thai", a change they do not see as a particular disaster although they are proud of their traditions and way of life when they stay in the mountains. Nonetheless, they feel that they are poor and powerless and that their best chance of escaping this condition may be to move out of the hills.

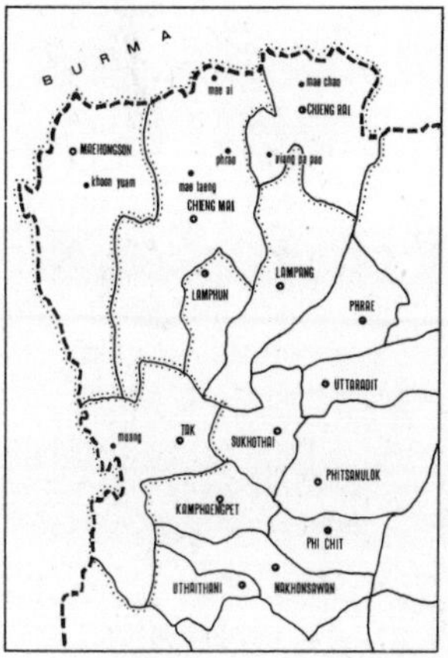

Total of villages :	*82*
Total of households :	*1,980*
Total population :	*12,545*

LISU

December flowers bloom on the hill slopes of Thailand's northern provinces and the mountain people tend the plants. But these are not innocuous blossoms - they are the opium poppies and those raising them may well be Lisu. The origins of these people go back to the Tibeto-Burman family of the Lolo group.

They once inhabited the land along the source of the Salween river in Tibet. Then they moved to Kachin in China's Yunnan province and the Shan States of present-day Burma. Some 70 years ago they moved again, this time to Thailand, to the mountain areas around Chiang Rai, Chiang

Lisu girls showing to full advantage the complexity of the design of their dresses.

A typical Lisu village set high in the hills.

Mai, Mae Hong Son and Tak, where some 12,500 Lisu, or Lisaw as the Shan and Thai call them, now reside.

The Lisu have a separate language, but can speak the tongues of the Lahu, Miao, Yunnanese and Shan - even if they cannot read and write their own language!

Housing

Lisu choose to build their houses on mountain tops, surrounded by a circle of mountains, to protect themselves and their kinsmen from possible enemies. The only entrance to their bamboo houses has a special name. In English it would be 'The exit of the spirit' and leads into a hut built low on the ground, the only raised part being the sleeping area which is raised one to two feet above the ground. One custom is that a married daughter of the family is only allowed to pass through this doorway - and thus visit her parents in their home - if she is accompanied by her husband.

A kettle of tea is always ready on the hearth, placed, as in some of the other tribes covered, in the centre of the floor. This is to give an appropriate welcome to any visitor or for members of the family. Against a wall is a wooden shelf. This

The normal bamboo conduit for a village's water supply has been supplemented here by a modern factory-made pipe.

Vhilst the girls are dancing, men follow the dancers, singing and playing a musical instrument called a 'cue-bue'.

acts as an altar for the worship of the spirits of ancestors.

A visitor sleeping in a Lisu house may be woken by the house shaking! It is doubtless a horse scratching on the house post or the reverberation of pigs in their sty. Barn, pigsty, chicken coop and stable are all built immediately next to the house.

No motorised vehicles are to be found in a Lisu village - the pony is the only mode of transport. These hardy animals can go anywhere and carry not only the farmer but paddy and anything else that has to be taken from one place to another. Like most other hill tribes, Lisu make sure that their village is close to a mountain stream so that there is always water to hand. This is brought to the village along a conduit made of bamboo cut lengthwise. This conduit goes right through the village.

A better view of the 'cue-bue'. It is a three-stringed instrument, likened to the Northern Thai 'cuong'.

Food

Lisu still retain their Chinese eating tastes. They drink tea in Chinese fashion and use chopsticks for eating. They prefer their food to be bland rather than the strong, hot flavours favoured by most Thais. Their favourite dish is pork and they enjoy this cooked with cabbage and dried Chinese mustard. All households pickle surplus food whenever they can for use when fresh supplies are not available.

Although they produce a lot of opium they are not addicted to it as are Miao. The betel nut is the stimulant used by everyone and they are also

Young Lisu men with their shirts decorated with silver ornaments.

Hand-in-hand, the young Lisu men and women dance in a circle. The steps are quite intricate.

fond of alcohol.

Dress

Lisu attire is very vivid and ay. The colour are particularly striking and the folk-weave cloth intricately designed. Women wear a multicoloured knee-length blouse. This is often in white, green, blue, yellow, red and purple. A large turban headdress of black cloth worn by them is reminiscent of the head covering of many African tribes.

Under their turbans, the women part their hair in the middle, drawing it back. Wide-legged pants complete the costume As if this attire was not magnificent enough, they also have a ceremonial costume. The heavy ornamentations make it a valuable possession - a costume may cost them as much as 3,000 baht (US$ 150).

The men are not outshone for they dress very gaily too. And jewellery is not the sole perogative of the women. Like European gypsies they sport a single earring of a type similar to the women.

Love and Marriage

Below the twinkling stars
I come to meet you with my
Fine cloth and powdered face.

The night is late
And the old folk sleep happily in their beds.
They cannot hear the sweet melody
Of my 'cue bue' or the pound
Of your mortar - but heaven hears.

You are young and have a body purfumed
Like the fragrance of a 'cue ve' flower in bloom,
But like the 'cue ve' it needs an insect kiss -
One 'cue ve' is not for a single bee alone - and
One bee can kiss more than one flower.

Why should you be afraid of cock-feather
Or a soft down of cotton ...... ?

The greatest happiness
For man and women - Please make room

Lisu dancing at the New Year celebration.

At your side and I shall help you pound
No need to feel sorry
On the day that you marry ....

So starts a young Lisu man's courtship serenade to his beloved. The young girl must have gone through the *soom chieng* ceremony at about 15 of 16 years old to proclaim her of age to be married. At this ceremony, the village witch-doctor or exorcist will present her with a 'moon flower' or silver disc. Then the courtship may begin, and by custom it must commence at the rice mortar where the girl must pound the paddy until her suitor arrives.

He will come late at night when he hears the sound of her mortar and he will take his 'cue bue', a type of three-stringed lute, hurry to the girl and woo her with his sweet love song. He will help her with her task and at the same time make his intentions known to her. If she consents, the man will offer his bracelet an an engagement bond and they will arrage to elope. They will go to his house and there they will stay for three days before sending his parents to discuss with hers the wedding arrangements.

Once the 'business' has been completed, it is for the witch-doctor to choose an auspicious day for the wedding. The groom will slaughter some pigs for the wedding feast, the first day of the ceremonies. On the second day, the bride will slaughter a pig which she, like a Lahu girl, will have raised and fattened for this special day.

There are good auspicious days for weddings and there are ones that forbode ill. The witch-doctor is thus much in demand to choose a day such as the ox-day, dog-day, goat-day and rabbit-day. Less lucky, but still allowed if haste is called for, are small snake-day, monkey-day and rat-day. But under no circumstances may a wedding take

Lisu men and women enjoying themselves. The men are playing tribar instruments.

place on tiger-day, dragon-day, horse-day or pig-day.

It will be seen that these days are named in the same way as the Eastern zodiac signs for the 12-year cycle. All Lisu are animists, believing that spirits dwell everywhere - house, field, cemetary or forest - the choice of day is of utmost importance for the *oo du thae* or wedding ceremony.

Once the ceremony is over only hard work faces the new wife. Some girls are free to choose their own spouses, but whoever they choose they will be more of a slave than a conventional wife. In spite of the elaborate courtship and love songs, the wife becomes little more than a domestic animal purchased for the purpose of hard work - the man will have invested much money in the wedding fees.

A wife cannot make decisions, she may not go anywhere, she may not complain. Marriage is slavery for the whole of her life. If her husband dies, she must live with his parents. If she wishes to remarry, only these parents can make the decision. She belongs to her husband's family now. And the dowry or bride-price paid by the second husband will be even higher than that paid by the first. The bride price is called *yend hor.*

When a woman gives birth to a child, the husband hastily sends for the witch-doctor. When he arrives, he immediately performs a ceremony to exorsize the child of the evil spirits within it's body. He stamps his foot hard on the ground and the evil spirit departs, then a holy thread is tied around the baby's wrist. Now the new-born baby is a complete human being and is accepted into the Lisu household.

Also at the New Year, Lisu girls, in full dress, take part in a dance to pay homage to the spirit of the sky.

Perhaps these young men will be courting at the festivities. Their valuable trimmings should cause attraction.

The Motto of the Men

"Yee betor, Char yetor shar cha. Too bheeka."

This is the motto of Lisu men - and it could be the motto of men everywhere! "Every man should be skilled in the art of drinking tea, drinking liquor, eating and making love".......

How well they live up to their motto is another question, but they are certainly skilled in using a cross-bow and locally-made firearms. They use these weapons for shooting birds, wild pigs, squirrels or wild fowl. They love, too, to play the *cue bue,* the lute-like instrument which, with its monotonous cadence, provides music for dancing as well as courting.

Lore of the Spirits

Lisu, as has been seen, are animists. They believe that spirits are all around them everywhere they go. To keep these spirits content, yearly offerings must be made by the chief religious leader. This man is the ritual leader of the group and his duties are manifold. He must be able to perform all manner of occult science. He will preside over death, sickness and marriage rituals, and he must advise and choose on all religious matters.

The people believe, too, in lucky charms to keep their fortunes high. Women wear amulets around their necks or carry tokens in a pocket or Shan bag wherever they go.

New Year Festivities

Another Chinese custom followed by Lisu is the elaborate celebration of New Year. This is held on the same dates at the traditional Chinese New Year and many of its features take a similar form.

Celebrations last six days and are divided into two sections - the 'minor' and the 'major'. At this time villagers busy themselves in pounding glutinous rice to make cakes, pigs and chickens are killed and the noise of fire-crackers permiates the air throughout the whole of the festivities. The fire-creackers - and the firing of guns are to honour *Phi Fah,* the spirit of the sky.

For the first three days, casuarina branches are hung before some of the houses and from these cakes, joss sticks and beeswax candles are hung as offerings. At night, a large bonfire is lit and there is much dancing. There is dancing around the casuarina branch, round and round in circles until dawn. The girls dress in their best finery. They wear ceremonial dresses and decorate themselves in their best jewellery - earrings, bracelets, bead necklaces and magnificent silver breast ornaments.

To welcome visitors, a wayside shelter is built of bamboo and wood, with its floor raised above the ground. Weary travellers can use this shelter after a long journey or it may be used by those returning from work in the fields. It is also used when there is sickness in the village. Inside the shelter, joints of bamboo, filled with water, are left for the thirsty. In the centre of the shelter hangs a white paper flag.

Dance of Sacrifice

Everyone in the village goes to the dance of sacrifice - *tieo ko* or *eia ya hma*. This, it is held, will bring good luck and prosperity to the village. Neighbours are called to join the dance with shouts of *'Tahoe siayia'* called out from time to time. Anyone adverse of joining in the merry making will have water thrown over them or their face may be rubbed with black soot from the cooking pot. The reticent person will be made to drink and join in the dancing.

Two special games are played which children the world over will recognise. One is hide-and-seek and the second is bag throwing. Young men and women stand facing one another and each takes turns to throw a bag. Anyone failing to catch it must pay a forfeit. The winner receives money or a gift in kind.

If the man loses he pays money, if the girl - she gives pipe tobacco. It may be thought that the girl always wins out, but no - it could be that her partner is not being strictly honest! He may insist on a rendez-vous in a secret place to pay her debt and if she falls for this age-old trick when she 'innocently' arrives at the chosen spot, he will give another type of reward, the *'ngo noe yi sheia'* - which means 'I love you' - and will then take her to be his wife.

'God' fathers

When a baby is a year old, his or her parents seek out a man to act as 'god' father. In fact this man becomes the foster parent and makes his pledge to the parents by tying two or three coins around the wrist of the child. This is a token that he has accepted the responsibility of becoming a father to the child. The real parents present him with a chicken and he is welcomed as a member of the family and is called the *shingchia.*

Death

Funerals are formal affairs and the etiquette of the event strictly kept. The dead person is dressed in both old and new clothes and at the head of the coffin are placed joss sticks, beeswax candles, a cup of tea, a cup of liquor and food.

It it is a child that has died, a chicken is slaughtered; a teenager, an average sized pig and for an adult, a large pig. The number of chickens or pigs is increased according to the number of days the corpse remains unburied.

The coffin is roughly hewn by family and neighbours. A large log is split into planks using a steel or wooden wedge. The planks are then bolted together with wooden nails. The funeral procession is led by the witch-doctor carrying a bag of the dead person's clothes on his shoulder and a white paper flag in one hand.

A death in a wealthy family is an occasion for a real wake. The family entertain lavishly and mourners cry in turn. Anyone not crying is thought to be unfaithful. The richer the person, the more clothes he will have had and if there are too many for the witch-doctor to carry, these will be sent to the burial ground on the back of a mule or a bull before the procession. At the cemetary, crackers or the firing of a gun announce to heaven that the dead person is coming. The clothes are laid in the grave with the coffin, the head being higher than the feet. After the grave has been covered with earth, the witch-doctor chants a farewell and relatives pay homage.

They will continue to make offerings to the deceased for three years. By that time, they believe, the soul will have been reborn.

An elderly Lisu woman smiles at visitors arriving at her village.

Land and skills

Lisu livelihood is agriculture. The tools they use are few in number and easy to repair. There is a large knife for cutting trees, a metal digging stick, a weeding tool and a metal sickle. All that is needed to make new ones or repair others are bellows, hammer and anvil. In this present age, however, some tools are bought in the district market.

Farming methods are primitive. No fertilizer is used except ash from burned forest cover or maize stubble. There is no attempt to enrich fields by putting animals out to pasture even though there is plenty of manure from domestic animals in the village.

Rice is the principal crop. Clearing starts in mid-January, big trees are cut in February and allowed to dry for about a month. As in some of the other tribes, the witch-doctor is the person who chooses the best day for the trees and shrub to be burned. Root crops are planted and unburned logs gathered and quickly disposed of so that rice planting may begin before the onset of the monsoon rains in May.

Chinese mustard and the maize ripen first and the others follow in season

Opium Poppy

Opium poppy growing begins when other

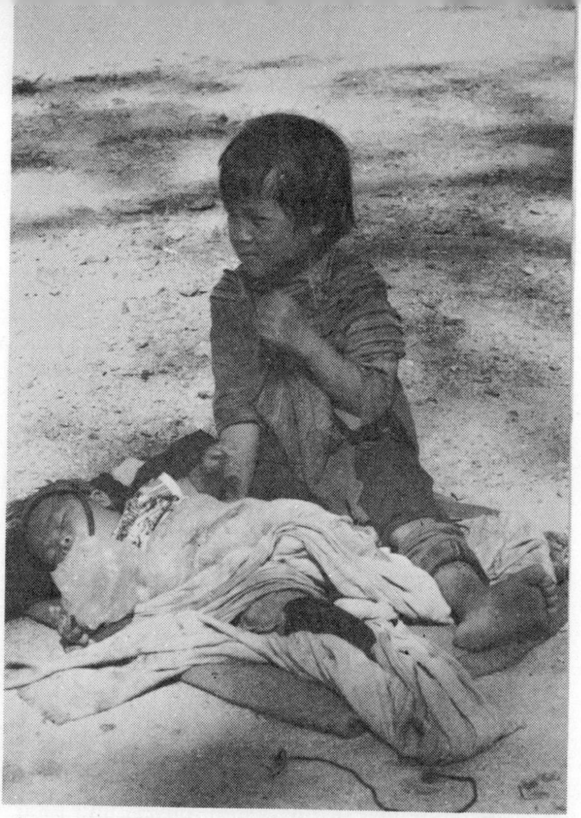

A very Lisu young girl baby sits for her even younger sister whilst the parents are out in the fields.

crops have all been harvested. Maize stubble is the best fertilizer. About December, on mountain slopes nurtured by warm, light sunshine, the poppies blossom. They are an awe-inspiring sight - flowers of purple and white cover the hill sides in their millions as far as the eye can see. A stranger to these parts will be astounded at the splendour and Lisu will be counting the great profit that the plant will bring.

When the petals start to fall after about four months, the fruit - rather like a teak nut - bears between five and ten nuts. In size they are similar to the lemon or betel nut. The leaves are like those of the green mustard. When the time for collecting the juice comes it is often the whole family who will move out into the fields to work throughout the season. The women collect the juice by using a cutting knife and a flat metal plate or bamboo skin.

The cutting knife resembles a sickle, but is much smaller. Some knives have single blades, others two or three, the tip being sharply curved. A cut is made upwards and the juice gathered from the fruit. It turns from a translucent colour to dark brown. The collecting season is the busiest time for all.

At the selling of the opium, buyers and food hawkers crowd in as if it were the celebration of some important festival. Under the light morning sunshine can be seen Yunnanese or northern Thai merchants laden with vermicelli roaming around the poppy fields. The vermicelli is sold both for cash or exchanged for raw opium.

Because Lisu start work early and it is inconvenient for them to cook food the opium collectors prefer to eat whilst working and this is a good chance for the food vendors to earn their income in an unusual way.

The ripe poppy is tapped three times, and

each milking has a different name. The first is *'yar hua'* or *'yar chao'*; the second is *'yar klarng'* and the last one is *'yar lar'* or *'yar harng'*. Naturally, each time the poppy is tapped, the quality is reduced. Once the juice has been collected the opium will be sold to the various types of traders who visit the scene.

Again, efforts are being made to encourage Lisu to change to a less harmful crop, but old habits die hard.....

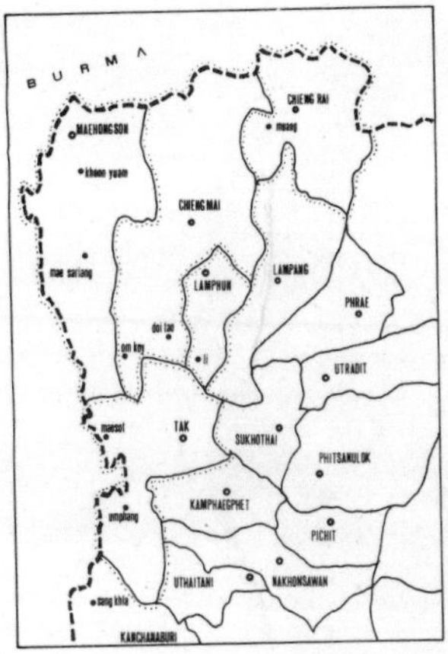

Total of villages :	*1,545*
Total of households :	*35,634*
Total population :	*184,648*

KAREN

Karen are a partly mountainous people of Tibeto-Burman ethnic stock, living mainly in south east Burma extending into the plain of Tenasserim. Their capital is Papun. They also live in the jungle and hills in the eastern frontier area of Burma and in the western part of Thailand.

Karen are divided into many groups, but those in Thailand may be classified into four ethnic divisions - Sakaw, P'wo, Bhew and Taungthu or Taungsu. They live along valleys surrounded by hills or mountains or near forest or streams. Some groups live on small hills and there are in the region of more than 184,000 in Thailand.

Karen tend their growing crops.

One type of Karen in native dress. They live peacefully and are very industrious.

They live mainly in the provinces of Mae Hong Son, Tak, and Kanchanaburi and scattered in the provinces of Chieng Rai, Lamphun, Lampang, Prae and Chiang Mai as well as parts of central Thailand.

They regard people of all nations as being born from the same bottle gourd. Karens were the first born and are thus the eldest - others coming later are deemed the younger ones.

Social Structure

Karens have an equitable temperament and are not savage or arrogant. They can justly be termed gentle. They live peacefully and are very industrious, honest and faithful. Their social structure and settlement patterns are well adapted for the occupation of all available land both through their ability to redistribute population by means of village exagamous marriage and through their willingness, both as individuals or as family units, to move away from their relatives.

Among Karen, as with Lawa, Yao and Miao, the basic unit of social structure is the household. Ideally these are composed of husband, wife and unmarried children together with a married daughter, husband and their children. In the hills, the ideal of the young married couple setting up home with the girl's parents seems to be adhered to quite closely. A man should live with his in-laws for at least two to three years before building his own home or returning with his wife to his native village. All Karen couples reported that their initial home after marriage was with the bride's father and very few couples reported moving to the husband's village after only a short period of living in this way.

In the ordinary pattern, no more than two married couples live in the same household. Usually it will be the youngest daughter and her husband who remain to care for her parents and who get a larger share of real property inheritance as a result.

Ancestral Spirits

Affiliation with ancestral spirits is determined by descent, not by residence, as with Lawa. Both men and women inherit their responsibilities towards ancestral spirits, their potential positions of religious leadership and their use-rights to cultivation in upland fields, as well as property rights, from their parents. The position regarding inheritance is made a little confused when the following factors are taken into consideration : religious change, scarcity of land and lack of suitable heirs for the position of religious leadership.

Religious Variability

Religious variability and change is characteristic of Karen - there being various religious traditions available as alternatives. These include a form of ancestral worship, *awxe;* tattooing, known in Karen as *cekosi;* one or other form of Christianity, usually Baptist or Catholic, and Buddhism. The last is particularly strong in Lamphun's Amphoe Li, where there are a large group supporting Khru Bar Wong. This project is actively aided by H.M. the King. The group, numbering several thousand, moved to Li from Chiang Mai's Doi Tao district where until some 20 years ago they actively aided Khru Bar Khow Phi, a disciple of the famous Khru Bar Sri Vichai.

The choice of any of these alternatives has important consequences for the structure of the family, extended kinship ties and the structure of village leadership. Ancestor worship, or rather the feeding of the spirits of the ancestors, is viewed by many Karen as a particularly onerous task. In order to fulfil the requirements of the ceremony, the family must raise special pigs and chickens for ceremonial use only. These must be replaced if they die before they are required. It is also necessary for every child of the ancestor whose spirit is being fed to participate in the ceremony. Thus sons who have gone to other villages must be summoned back for the special ritual.

Because of these and similar requirements, many families have decided to give up the service of their ancestral spirits and this they do by undergoing a tattooing ceremony. The purported purpose of this is to 'kill' or permanently satisfy the desires of the ancestral spirits. If some of the children do this and others do not, there is inevitably a split in the family unit since members of the group which communally makes a sacrifice to ancestral spirits may share in certain kinds of sacrificial meals.

It is pertinent to note at this point that the large group of Karen Buddhists previously mentioned are strict vegetarians and will not even eat eggs, let alone meat or fish.

Individuals who become tattooed usually

explain their action on the basis of convenience : they are relieved of the task of raising special animals for eventual sacritice or seeking them whenever their ancestral spirits demand to be fed. And they also believe that by satisfying permanently the desires of the ancestral spirits, they will no longer be subject to sicknesses caused by them. Another reason for conversion is that it is difficult or impossible to follow different traditions within the same household especially when the groom sets up in his wife's father's house and must conform to or convert to her traditions. This is hard as an ancestor worshipping person cannot eat sacrificial meals with those who accept the authority of a tattooed religious leader. This is just one feature which has affected the inheritance of religious positions and thus forms the basis for schisms within the community.

Conversion to Christianity, of course, has the same effect since religious leadership of the community is based on the ability, willingness and having the qualifications to feed just those spirits which are thought to affect the well-being of the community as a whole.

Scarcity of land also reinforces the problem of religious differences. In the normal operation of the Karen inheritance system, conflict must eventually occur over the legitimate inheritance of the position of religious leadership. Under the normal circumstances of an expanding population,

The Karen girl on the right has a splendid collection of bracelets.

the solution to this difficulty should be for one or other of the contenders to the position of religious leader to found another community or colony, taking with him as many of his followers as he can collect. However, under the present system this becomes impossible since there is

Karens rest by the roadside after a visit to market.

insufficient land available for this. Thus a schism, once in going, finds no easy solution.

One of the paramount rules of Karen behaviour with respect to relatives is that one cannot accept the authority of a younger sibling or anyone classified as a younger sibling. The classification of seniority has been widely extended, in fact it can be extended to anyone living within the community or even to any Karen. It is possible to express the relationship between two Karens in a community in terms of being 'younger brother' or 'elder brother' or younger or elder cousin on one or other rule. But the rules may be ambiguous when they are applied to people who are not real siblings. There are many rules of a similar nature. Given these rules which they say they should follow, communities must be unstable. This helps to account for the great range in size of Karen communities and for the speed with which Karens have spread themselves in north-west Thailand.

Co-operation Between Households

Obligations for mutual assistance between households are much less formally structured among Karen than in other tribes. This is related to the absence of clearly defined descent groupings and to their presence among other hill tribes. Households of siblings usually assist each other in the heavy tasks of farming, but there is no obligation to provide a share of sacrificial liquor, as among Lawa. In spite of the fact of formal obligation, relatives and children who have married outside the village often appear at planting or harvest time to help. Otherwise, co-operative labour is on an arranged basis where a day's work is repaid with a day's work.

A set of siblings, or parents and their children may form an informal co-operative group and houses in a village may be grouped into areas of households related in this way. In some villages, these are not permanent. At a minimum, such a grouping is a matter of convenience in caring for aged parents.

According to Karen belief, the house belongs to its owner, even after he dies - and thus must be abandoned or destroyed on his death. The owner is, in fact, normally the female head of the household and thus in villages are found old widows living in small houses near their children with whom they eat and in whose fields they continue to work for as long as they are able.

Agricultural rituals are supposed to be conducted within the group according to the order of seniority within the group. This affects, to a certain extent, the order in which agricultural work will be done, where order of seniority within a group takes priority.

Marriage and Sexual Mores

Marriage among Karen is usually for life. Divorce is very rare and strongly disapproved of. Plural marriage by either sex is not permitted. A widow or widower may, however, remarry.

A young courting man does not go into the girl's house but creeps under the floor where the girl sleeps and puts his hand through a hole in the floor to awaken her. In every house where there is a daughter of marriageable age, such a hole is specially arranged for the girl's lover. When she learns of his interest from contact made

A Karen women dressed in her finery makes an attractive picture against the background of her village.

through the floor, she opens the door and willingly comes out to meet him. Later on there will be a formal engagement and wedding. On the wedding night the bride and groom feed rice and chicken to each other.

Marriage of a man to someone classified as 'older cousin' is not permitted. Sexual intercourse is supposed to be confined to marriage, but premaritial sexual relationships do take place, usually resulting in marriage. Of 32 male heads of households questioned, seven reported having paid at the time of their wedding the fine required of those who have had premarital sexual relations. Several people were also said to have violated rules governing marriage between certain kinsfolk. Karen do not believe, as do Lawa, that an 'incestuous' marriage will result in the birth of a malevolent spirit *(phi ka).* Thus the couple concerned are not driven from the village.

Adultery, on the other hand, is supposed to induce the wrath of the earth spirits and requires a sacrifice of a large animal, such as a pig or buffalo, to be paid for by the offending parties, plus a ritual distribution by them of salt to each household in the village. The entire household - if one of the parties in the act is considered more responsible for what has taken place - or of both parties - if each are held equally responsible - are driven from the village to prevent disaster in the form of disease or crop failure.

Young Karen singing and playing musical instruments during a wedding ceremony.

A situation of this type occurred in a particular Karen village. After several months of debate and the payment of fines, the offending woman and her household left the village. The man in the case, who claimed to have been seduced, did not leave but found it very difficult to get help in planting, weeding and harvesting his crops.

A young Karen man makes melodious music to attract his sweetheart

Another family, including one of the sisters of the offending woman, left the village soon after the case began to be discussed for fear that disaster would come to the village. It can be seen that rules controlling sexual behaviour are another mechanism for the dispersal of the Karen population.

Religious Leadership

Each village should have a religious leader whose duty is to deal with the most important and dangerous spirits. This man is known as *'thipokawkesa'*. Only he has the power and courage to address offerings to this type of spirit. If he is unsuccessful, his followers may leave him. He will probably have inherited the position from his father. It is unclear what happens when a witch-doctor dies without a male heir.

The *thipokawkesa* should have a helper - the two are sometimes referred to as 'head' and 'tail'. The helper will also be a descendant in the male line of a founding, but separate, family. The helper can officiate at less important functions. Although the witch-doctor inherits his position, his status is secure only if he and his followers are successful. He should be rich and generous - his followers may interpret contrary indications to show that the spirits do not look with favour on him. Unlike Lawa, his position is not based clearly on descent from nobility and his function does not include the final interpretation of Karen customs and tradition. The writer knows of one case where the witch-doctor was severely criticized at a ritual by those who thought he was soliciting too much money for the sacrificial animal. They contended that if he were a proper *thipokawkesa* he should have been able to make a large contribution himself and his poverty proved to them that he was not the proper person for the job.

Civil Leadership

It is common for civil headmen of Karen hill villages to have responsibility for several small villages, dispersed over a large area. Such a headman is recognised by district (amphoe) officials. Decisions affecting the village are made at meetings of heads of households called by the headman and held at his house. Women sometimes attend these meetings and may speak at them. Some villages, however, are not well organized to perform community tasks. In these cases it is usually public opinion that is the arbiter of decisions.

Law and Order

Petty theft of tools or garden produce is common - often the suspected persons are opium users or addicts. Little is done, however, other than gossip to control the behaviour of wrongdoers. The headman warns of the illegality of opium smoking, but it has not been publicly or officially condemned.

Village fights are common - usually following drinking at some ceremony or other. In some villages no action is taken to stop the dispute, nor are fines assessed for wrong doers.

Making a Living

The economy of Karen of most villages is essentially similar to other hill tribes. All households in the village are directly dependent on agriculture for subsistence. Upland farming follows a pattern of one year of cultivation followed by six to 10 years of fallow, but the increase in population is shortening the fallow time. Elders in the village can clearly see the decline in yields which results from this shortened fallow time.

A Karen woman seen with the family pig.

Few villagers make winter gardens, preferring to buy vegetables as, they contend, garden produce may be stolen. They also tend to plant fewer fruit trees for the same reason and also because they do not expect to spend their whole lives in the same village. Many rely on forest greenstuff when it is in season. Those living in the hills are less inclined to build permanent houses and for those they do build, split bamboo is used for siding and flooring rather than wooden planks.

They are mostly subsistence rice cultivators. Some households own elephants or shares in elephants and these animals are used in the rainy and cool seasons for low land lumber work. Some Karen in Mae Sariang have even worked in the mines.

The Outside World

For at least 100 years Karens have had trade and administrative relations with the valley-based northern Thai. Burmese-Karen relations have nearly always been much more hostile than Thai-Lawa or Thai-Karen contacts.

The primary mark of ethnic identity for Karen seems to be language and they frequently comment that they do not like to speak Northern Thai even though they often know some of it. They will not do so unless they absolutely have to. Many who aspire to be literate want to read and write Karen so that they can send love letters to friends in other villages.

The Karen headman is responsible for ensuring that government records are kept up-to-date and that taxes due are collected. Villagers are taxed on their upland fields, guns and liquor distilling. They are also supposed to pay registration fees for irrigated field-titles, buffaloes, elephants and identity cards.

Families, excepting old widows, are dependent on trade with lowland Thais. The most common item is rice which is also the chief item of trade with other upland villagers. There is also a little trade with nearby Lawa villagers who come to get chickens, piglets and the dogs for their particular ceremonies and diet. Money, husked rice, vegetables, liquor or yeast are given in return. Craft specialities are also traded to villages which do not have either the raw materials or skill. When dealing with the lowland peoples, those who have much surplus rice trade with relatives or other Karens in their area. When buying things they usually prefer dealing with Karen-speaking traders. It could be that they are shy with the ordinary Thai. An English monk, who was abbot of a temple in a mainly Karen area, reports on many interesting Buddha Dhamma and other discussions with a strange mixture of English, Northern Thai and Karen languages.

Rice or money is usually borrowed from relatives, neighbours or those from nearly villages.

An unmarried Karen girl, who traditionally, must wear white. The dress is ankle length.

The interest rate at any time before harvest is 50 per cent! Loans for larger amounts are often secured with a mortgage on the borrower's irrigated fields - if he happens to own one. Interest rates seem unrelated to market conditions.

Spokesman

The desire to have a spokesman in an unfamiliar official situation is characteristic of Karen and all other hill tribes, Anyone who is assumed to be more powerful - whatever his calling - will be pressed into service for this purpose and, without such an intermediary, hill people are very reluctant to seek services from lowland authorities.

In general, Karen do not take an open attitude with respect to the outside world. They define their world as a Karen world in which the boundaries between ethnic groups are or should be closed.

Conclusion

The hill Karens living in remote villages are faced with problems very similar to those of Yao, Miao, Akha, Lawa, Lahu and Lisu. The major problems are economic and demographic.

Their population is expanding rapidly at the same time as their resource base is remaining constant or declining. There is no immediate prospect for change in their agricultural economy. A more lasting solution to the problem of cash income must be sought in diversified sources.

The agricultural situation will probably become serious with the next few years so that efforts should be directed toward the development of improved upland farming methods in order to avert further rapid deterioration of soil and watershed resources and widespread malnutrition.